ROLL TIDE WEST COAST

FORWARD PASS OFFENSE

FOOTBALL'S
GAME CHANGERS

ZONE BLITZES

MONDAY WALTER

NIGHT CAMP

ICONS, RECORD BREAKERS, SCANDALS, SUPER BOWLS, AND MORE

DEACON BOWL GAMES
JONES

W9-CPE-506

FOOTBALL'S
GAME CHANGERS
Icons, Record Breakers, Scandals, Super Bowls, and More

BARRY WILNER AND KEN RAPPOPORT

GUILFORD, CONNECTICUT

To Helene, the best there has ever been. Stay strong.
—Barry

For Madeleine. Welcome to the family.
—Ken

An imprint of Rowman & Littlefield

Distributed by NATIONAL BOOK NETWORK

Copyright © 2016 by Barry Wilner and Ken Rappoport

All rights reserved. No part of this book may be reproduced in any form or by any electronic or mechanical means, including information storage and retrieval systems, without written permission from the publisher, except by a reviewer who may quote passages in a review.

British Library Cataloguing in Publication Information Available

Library of Congress Cataloging-in-Publication Data is available on file.

ISBN 978-1-4930-2421-6
ISBN 978-1-4930-2422-3 (e-book)

∞™ The paper used in this publication meets the minimum requirements of American National Standard for Information Sciences—Permanence of Paper for Printed Library Materials, ANSI/NISO Z39.48-1992.

CONTENTS

INTRODUCTION

Football is America's Game. There's no denying it these days.

The Super Bowl is akin to a national holiday. Bowl games, particularly the major ones such as the Rose, Orange, Sugar, Cotton, and Fiesta, are celebrations of the college gridiron.

The NFL is the king of television—and not just because its games outdraw just about anything else on the tube. Even the league's draft is popular enough that two networks carry it live, from first pick to Mr. Irrelevant—No. 256.

Fantasy football has taken America by storm, adding to the gambling (legal and otherwise) on the outcomes of games, and to the wagering that ranges from the mundane point spread to the exotic, such as who will win the Super Bowl coin toss.

Now that college football has a playoff, instituted in 2014, a true champion should be the result—although with a committee of "experts" deciding which four teams get into the playoff, objectivity still could take a holiday. In any event, the first two championship games under the new system drew 33.4 million viewers and 25.7 million viewers, respectively.

But football wasn't always so popular. Not even close.

The authors of *Football's Game Changers* have examined the gridiron game from the day it was invented—there are even some arguments over when and where that occurred—right up to recent NFL scandals. Along the way, we found the heroes and villains of the sport; the power brokers and the fools; the dynasties and the one-shot ponies.

The game changers chosen for the 50 chapters of this book reflect on every crucial aspect of the sport. Yes, the good, the bad, and the ugly.

More than 100 years ago, the very existence of football was threatened by its violent nature and the injuries and deaths it caused. President Theodore Roosevelt intervened, rules were developed, equipment was improved, and, through the years, the game's popularity grew.

Roosevelt might not have been football's first game changer, but he could have been the most important, and his role is detailed herein.

Throughout the decades, the game has grown because of the people on the field playing it, those on the sidelines coaching it, and the administrators charged with its development. *Football's Game Changers* is filled with the people who made an unmistakable and irreplaceable impact, and their stories, along with the scandals and controversies that permeate football today.

The Pioneers: John Heisman, Amos Alonzo Stagg, Pop Warner, and Walter Camp. What they did helped make football what it is today.

Legendary Coaches: Knute Rockne (1920s) and Vince Lombardi (1960s) dominated football during their time; Paul Brown; Bear Bryant; Joe Paterno and his "Grand Experiment"; and Eddie Robinson, the Martin Luther King of black football. Their leadership skills were legendary.

African-American Breakthrough: Marion Motley, Kenny Washington, Woody Strode, and Bill Willis reintegrated professional football after a 12-year absence of African Americans.

AUDIBLE

"I believe in outdoor games, and I do not mind in the least that they are rough games, or that those who take part in them are occasionally injured. I have no sympathy whatever with the overwrought sentimentality that would keep a young man in cotton wool, and I have a hearty contempt for him if he counts a broken arm or collar bone as of serious consequence when balanced against the chance of showing that he possesses hardihood, physical address, and courage. But when these injuries are inflicted by others, either wantonly or of set design, we are confronted by the question not of damage to one man's body, but of damage to the other man's character. Brutality playing a game should awaken the heartiest and most plainly shown contempt for the player guilty of it, especially if this brutality is coupled with a low cunning in committing it without getting caught by the umpire." —*President Theodore Roosevelt on "rough" football as opposed to "brutal" football, June 1905, at a Harvard alumni event*

How football has changed from the game as played here, in the 1920s

Superstars like Jim Brown and Deacon Jones followed. They helped open the doors for thousands of minority players, coaches, and front office personnel.

Great Administrators and Owners: Includes hands-down the best commissioner of any sport, Pete Rozelle, one of the central figures in the AFL-NFL merger, as well as owners "Papa Bear" George Halas, Wellington Mara, Art Rooney, and Al Davis, the rebel with a cause.

Brilliant Innovators: Roone Arledge and Tony Verna, who brought *Monday Night Football* and instant replay to the game.

Controversies and Scandals: The Patriots breaking rules and winning championships; the concussion dilemma; the betting scandals; the Penn State scandal; countless off-the-field problems facing commissioner Roger Goodell; and many others are featured in this book.

The Magnificent Players: Magical names that conjure up magical deeds: the Four Horsemen; Red Grange, the "Galloping Ghost"; Slingin' Sammy Baugh; and Chuck "Concrete Charlie" Bednarik, the last of the two-way players. Among the other giants who built the game: Otto Graham, Sid Luckman, Dick Butkus, John Unitas, Lance Alworth, and Jim Parker. For argument's sake, how do you think Unitas, who once held the record with 47 straight games with TD passes, would match up in a battle with great quarterbacks, such as Tom Brady?

How would Grange, the first college football superstar, do in a test of great running backs against Adrian Peterson?

How many of today's best linebackers can match skills with Bednarik?

While it's acknowledged that players today are bigger, faster, and stronger, are they more talented? One can argue which decade featured the best players. Here are some to consider:

From the 1970s: Mean Joe Greene, Terry Bradshaw, Roger Staubach, Jack Lambert, John Hannah, Ted Hendricks, and Franco Harris.

From the 1980s: Joe Montana, Walter Payton, Lawrence Taylor, Jerry Rice, Reggie White, Anthony Munoz, Mike Singletary, Darrell Green, and Eric Dickerson.

From the 1990s: Brett Favre, Emmitt Smith, Bruce Smith, Barry Sanders, Deion Sanders, John Elway, Rod Woodson, and Derrick Thomas.

From the New Millennium: Tom Brady, Peyton Manning, Aaron Rodgers, Ray Lewis, Tony Gonzalez, Curtis Martin, Junior Seau, Jonathan Ogden, and Marshall Faulk.

Greatness everywhere. Football at its finest, from the beginning to the present.

Greatness everywhere. Football at its finest, from the beginning to the present.

Here in *Football's Game Changers*, the authors have selected their 50 most influential forces in football history. Enjoy for a leisurely read, or take notes for some competitive argument-settling.

Television

The Tube Makes Football America's Game

Pro football owes the majority of its success to television. As far back as the early 1960s, Commissioner Pete Rozelle recognized that it would be so. And so did the sport's influential owners.

Their successors, whether overseeing franchises or the league itself, have followed suit in pursuing every penny potential broadcast partners could offer. Indeed, when Fox came around in 1994, the network's stunning $1.58 billion deal with the NFL provided that network with a cachet it might never have gotten.

At the time, Fox had only 140 stations, of which 120 were UHF and not as readily available across the nation as CBS and NBC. Fox also had no sports department and no history in sports.

NO. 5

"We'll do it better," Lucie Salhany, the chairman of Fox, promised at the time. "It'll be first class. We want to make the NFL look better than what we've seen. We have the crown jewel of all sports."

That the NFL was No. 1 had become clear many years earlier when pro football surpassed baseball as America's top sport. Yet the NFL was willing to dump longtime partner CBS—which soon enough would return to the fold and remain there—and show faith that Fox would take off. It certainly did, with NFL programming as the catalyst.

Fox got into the NFL business long after the league had become must-see television.

The 1958 NFL title match at Yankee Stadium between the Baltimore Colts and New York Giants, dubbed "The Greatest Game Ever Played," was the first in league history to go into overtime. A national TV audience of 45 million watched on NBC, and the Colts' dramatic victory whetted their appetite for more small-screen gridiron.

It also piqued the interest of one Lamar Hunt, son of Texas oil millionaire H. L. Hunt.

"My interest emotionally was always more in football," he said. "But clearly the '58 Colts-Giants game, sort of in my mind, made me say, 'Well, that's it. This sport really has everything. And it televises well.' And who knew what that meant?"

Every pro football team owner, which would include Hunt very soon after that legendary game, grew to know what that meant.

Now ubiquitous: a television camera on a mobile platform used for sideline shots

The merger of the AFL and NFL really changed the landscape, particularly when they became one league in 1970 after three seasons of playing apart, except for the championship game that became known as the Super Bowl. Before then, the asking price—some say the begging price because Rozelle actually had to recruit broadcast partners in the early 1960s—was $600,000 for the entire season. That's what CBS paid.

Those numbers increased significantly throughout the NFL's war with the AFL, going up to $4.65 million for the 1962-63 season, then to $28.2 million for the next two campaigns. But it was in 1966, when the merger was first struck, that the NFL got its initial long-term deal with the network: $75.2 million for four years.

Meanwhile, TV would prove critical to pro football prospering and the eventual merger.

At the outset, the AFL had a deal with ABC, which lagged well behind CBS and NBC in programming and attractiveness. Each of the eight teams received about $100,000 in 1960, but the payments decreased the next season because of low advertising revenues.

Still, the AFL was on par with the big boys by having a presence on the tube. And in a brilliant marketing move, the AFL allowed broadcasts in the home cities of out-of-market games while following the lead of the NFL on blacking out a team at home. So if the Chargers were at the Jets, New York would instead get Patriots-Bills, for example. That ensured TV time every Sunday. "The ABC contract right off the bat helped with the exposure, and it was very important to the success of the AFL," said Barron Hilton, the original owner of the Chargers.

Just as the NFL built off the 1958 Colts-Giants classic, the AFL got its legendary game in 1962. Not just one overtime, but a pair between the two-time defending champion Houston Oilers and Hunt's Dallas Texans. The Texans even botched the OT coin toss when star running back Abner Haynes misunderstood coach Hank Stram's instructions and chose to kick into a brisk wind. The Texans survived that blunder, and even though they high-tailed out of Dallas for Kansas City the next year, the AFL was building a decent national following.

The AFL got its legendary game in 1962. Not just one overtime, but a pair between the two-time defending champion Houston Oilers and Hunt's Dallas Texans.

"It was a newsworthy event," Hunt said. "A longer game than any other in pro football, and it was the AFL championship game. It was very memorable, and a lot of people saw it."

That the league played wide-open, high-scoring, pass-oriented football also made it more popular than any previous challenger to the NFL.

Wisely, for the second successive season, the AFL scheduled its 1963 title match on a day the NFL was not playing its championship game. San Diego routed the Patriots 51–10.

"People watched that game because they wanted to see football," said Al LoCasale, an AFL executive who worked for the Chargers and Raiders. "And it had a vast audience of people who did not have familiarity with the AFL."

Heading toward the 1964 season, Rozelle, who would soon become the most powerful person in sports, was in a can't-lose position. His league's TV rights were up for bidding, and all three networks wanted a piece.

ABC, willing to dump the AFL for the more-established organization, bid $9.3 million for two years of NFL coverage. Then NBC's bid was unveiled, and it far surpassed ABC's offer. Finally, Rozelle opened the CBS offer: $28.2 million for two seasons.

There was another winner, too. The AFL knew that NBC desperately wanted in on the pro game. Sonny Werblin, who had taken over the New York franchise and renamed it from Titans to Jets, previously had been on the other side of the table as a TV executive. He knew how to extract every possible penny from the networks, and he closed a $36 million agreement for five years with NBC—$850,000 per AFL franchise.

"In 1965, when NBC got the rights, that gave every club sufficient funds to where they could all be profitable from that point on," Hilton said. "We were all elated to get with NBC."

When that contract was concluded, there was a tidal wave of reaction throughout the NFL, whose franchises had once believed the AFL would soon be extinct. Not anymore.

"Our owners realized they were not going away when NBC signed them to a new, big-money contract," said Joe Browne, Rozelle's right-hand man. "They had economic stability with that TV money."

Indeed, economic stability would never be a concern again for pro football teams. Rights fees skyrocketed through every negotiation. When the merger took full form in 1970, all three

On Football's Importance to Television

"Football is the defining point of any network. . . . the only firm ground in an increasingly scary swamp as we look at the future of television. It is the one thing that makes sense. Shows have a life cycle. The NFL has gone on for . . . years." —*Fox Sports president David Hill*

AUDIBLE

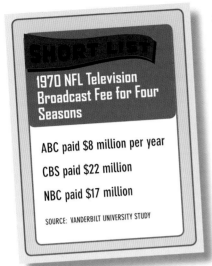

SHORT LIST

1970 NFL Television Broadcast Fee for Four Seasons

ABC paid $8 million per year

CBS paid $22 million

NBC paid $17 million

SOURCE: VANDERBILT UNIVERSITY STUDY

networks became league broadcast partners. Together, they spent aproximately $185 million for four seasons and, for the first time, there would be weekly games played on a day other than Sunday.

Rozelle championed the idea of Monday night contests, and ABC was more than ready to oblige. "There are a lot more TV sets in use on Monday night than on Sunday afternoon," Rozelle reasoned. "We're undoubtedly getting a lot of new fans."

How did that work out? *Monday Night Football* became a staple of fans' viewing and today, on ESPN, is the second-longest-running TV series behind CBS's *60 Minutes*.

That program also gave birth to "Dandy Don," "Giff," and "Humble Howard." No sports broadcasting team before or since had the impact on American culture that Don Meredith ("Turn out the lights, the party's over"), Frank Gifford, and Howard Cosell did. They joked, they bickered, they welcomed all kinds of celebrities to the booth. They tackled controversial issues. They made watching game highlights a pastime long before ESPN saw the light of day.

The program's creator, Roone Arledge, is considered a pioneer of sports TV. His greatest invention was MNF. Dick Ebersol, an Arledge protégé and eventually NBC Sports chairman, said of Arledge to the *New York Times*: "Roone was surely the only television executive of his time who would have dared to put sports in prime time. All of the money the athletes are making, all the big money in sports, none of that would be happening if not for Roone."

As TV ratings soared on Sundays and Monday nights, so did the rights fees. By the end of the 1970s, the NFL was raking in more than $160 million a year from the three networks. The next deal, for five seasons, brought the total revenue to more than a billion bucks for the first time: $1.89 billion as CBS carried the NFC, NBC had the AFC, and ABC had the prime-time showcase. All three rotated televising the Super Bowl.

Another innovation came in 1987 when ESPN, owned by ABC, dived in to show eight Sunday night games in the second half of the schedule—including exhibitions, ESPN got 39 games in the deal—for $153 million over three years. It marked the NFL's first journey onto cable TV. Astutely, the NFL insisted that the regular-season matches be shown on over-the-air free TV in the markets of the two participating teams.

In 1990: TNT joined the Sunday night party, sharing the schedule with ESPN as a full season of prime-time games now was televised on Sundays and Mondays.

Then came Fox's blockbuster in '94, with CBS getting shut out because it showed no interest in the AFC package. As the NFL raked in $4.388 billion for four seasons, NBC kept AFC rights, and the network associated with the NFL since 1960 was out.

Not for long, though. In the next negotiations, CBS secured the AFC away from NBC, which had become the "Olympic network" and couldn't justify the $4 billion expenditure required to stick with football. Meanwhile, advertisers were paying heavily to be involved in the telecasts. So much so that the cost of a 30-second commercial in the 2006 Super Bowl had reached $2.4 million. It would nearly double by 2015.

Always searching for more avenues to present the game on television, not to mention more revenues from the carriers, the NFL also signed up satellite network DIRECTV in 1998. DIRECTV offered a unique package to viewers who wanted to watch out-of-market teams, games unavailable on the networks except in the regions of teams involved. The price tag for Sunday Ticket: $400 million annually for six seasons. DIRECTV grew its offerings to the fans as it renewed with the NFL in 2004 for five years and for another four years in 2009, when it paid $1 billion annually. In 2014, that agreement was extended for eight seasons at an average of $1.5 billion a year, a 50 percent increase. Viewers had become enamored of the Red Zone Channel, which showed all scoring plays as well as forays inside the opponent's 20-yard line by every team. In 2015, DIRECTV also brought the NFL Mix, in which fans could watch either four or eight games on one screen.

In the decade since the 2005 contracts worth $22.4 billion over six years brought NBC in as the Sunday night carrier and put Monday nighters on cable's ESPN, the NFL had found new ways to bring the game to its ever-burgeoning fan base. Online streaming became popular enough that a game from London was broadcast that way alone, except in Buffalo and Jacksonville, the two cities whose teams played at Wembley Stadium in October 2015.

The cost of a 30-second commercial in the 2006 Super Bowl had reached $2.4 million. It would nearly double by 2015.

Thursday night games came to the tube in 2006, first limited to eight contests on the NFL Network, which launched in 2003. By 2014, CBS had upped their game for an expanded schedule so that every team played at least one Thursday contest per season.

TV revenues even had an impact on the ending of the league's 2011 lockout of the players from March to July. After the lockout was settled with a 10-year labor deal, ESPN plunked down $16 billion for eight years, then CBS, Fox, and NBC grabbed nine-year agreements for $1 billion a season.

Television is truly a golden goose—and the lifeblood of the NFL.

The Super Bowl

America's Biggest Annual Event (That Didn't Even Sell Out When It Started!)

Everyone watches the Super Bowl.

For avid football followers to occasional fans to the folks just there for the party, the Super Bowl has become sports' combination of Mardi Gras and New Year's Eve. It's must-see viewing, whether you're rooting for one of the teams; betting on one of them (or on some of the exotic wagers available); awaiting the halftime show; or just at a Super Bowl party for the good eating and clever (or unwatchable) commercials.

"The Super Bowl is a celebration of our great sport, and it's a celebration of the fans who support our great sport," Commissioner Roger Goodell said. "It's the culmination of the season and the reward for the hard work and dedication by the players and coaches and everyone in a team's organization."

NO. **4**

He stopped short of calling it the Greatest Show on Earth, but that's what Goodell and predecessors Pete Rozelle and Paul Tagliabue have sought since the merger was completed and the AFL-NFL Championship Game was invented in 1967. No, it wasn't called the Super Bowl back then, and it was anything but a can't-miss extravaganza. In fact, it didn't come close to selling out the seats at the stadium.

Rozelle, who remained commissioner of the combined leagues, had several fears about that first matchup, Vince Lombardi's dynastic Packers against AFL representative Kansas City.

He worried that the AFL teams couldn't compete with the established clubs of the NFL. He feared that fans and media wouldn't accept the title contest as a valid final event of the season if it wasn't competitive. He wondered if the franchises headed to the NFL—there were nine in the AFL when the first combined championship game was played and there would be 10 when the merger was completed in 1970 after Cincinnati came aboard—were financially stable enough.

Rozelle and his cohorts in the NFL tried to avoid any consideration that the Chiefs might

A golden ticket: Welcome to Super Bowl XLVI.

beat the Packers in that first title meeting. But they understood it was essential to stage such a game, though Rozelle initially balked when merger talks were close to completion.

And the pressure on Lombardi—if not his players, many of whom spent more time partying than practicing in California—was intense.

"He wasn't really nervous," said quarterback Bart Starr, the MVP of the Packers' 35–10 win over the Chiefs. "He was just trying to let us know we were representing the prestige of the NFL. There was great pride. He didn't want us to take that for granted. We were the league's first representative in that game."

Starr also believed the Chiefs didn't get their due as a worthy opponent.

"We recognized when we were preparing for the game just how good they were," Starr said. "Players and coaches knew and, just a few short years later, they had their moment in the sun when they beat Minnesota in Super Bowl IV."

Before getting there—and beyond to all the Super Bowl would become—there was the debut game on January 15, 1967, which drew a crowd of 61,946 to the 100,000-seat Los Angeles Coliseum. The media swarm was more like a casual gathering: 338 credentials as opposed to more than 6,300 nowadays.

Ticket prices? Rozelle worried that the NFL charged too much at a top price of $12. Three decades later, he told the *Los Angeles Times*: "This year, they're charging $12 for the game program."

And ticket prices would reach $500 for the cheapest seats at Super Bowl XLIX.

Green Bay's decisive victories in the first two AFL-NFL Championship Games—Oakland was the victim, 33–14, in 1968—satisfied the establishment, but diminished anticipation for the next one. Generally, the sporting public considered whoever won the NFL title to be the

On Super Bowl Goals

"Our goal from the first was to make this more than a game, to make it an event. That was because of the initial perception that the champion of the American Football League wouldn't be competitive with the National Football League champion. So we wanted an event, even if it wasn't a competitive game. We wanted people to have some fun." —*former commissioner Pete Rozelle*

AUDIBLE

champs. In a stroke of marketing genius, Rozelle adapted Chiefs owner Lamar Hunt's suggestion of naming the big game the Super Bowl. The ironies are aplenty and quite delicious:

- Rozelle thought the term was corny;
- The man who helped found the AFL and in great part kept it afloat during the 1960s until the merger agreement was responsible for such a brilliant maneuver, not someone from the establishment.

Hunt had gotten the idea from the Super Ball his daughter, Sharron, had been playing with. "I don't think you can place any credit for creativity on my part. It just came out," Hunt said of a meeting with the planning committee for the game.

Now that the game had, well, a Super name, it still was lacking in cachet. Heading into the 1969 match, the NFL's Baltimore Colts were 19-point favorites over the AFL's New York Jets. To the rescue: Broadway Joe (more in Game Changer 28).

Jets quarterback Joe Namath, already a massive personality in the Big Apple and outside of football for his outgoing personality, sometimes-outlandish off-field machinations (wearing fur coats, accompanying gorgeous women, endorsing all sorts of non-sports products), made his famous guarantee. Then he made good on it in a 16–7 shocker that wasn't nearly that close.

Suddenly, the little league-that-could had reached solid ground in the football world. Underdogs everywhere had their champion. And the AFL-NFL Championship Game was now Super.

"The game that made it what it is now was Super Bowl III, the Joe Namath game," Rozelle said in 1996. "When the AFL champions, Joe's New York Jets, showed they could not only play competitively but beat the NFL's best team, that set the pattern for the future."

Heading into the 1969 match, the NFL's Baltimore Colts were 19-point favorites over the AFL's New York Jets.

It hasn't stopped. Through the perfect Dolphins of 1972, still the only club to be spotless and win the title, to the Steel Curtain dynasty. From the Silver and Black out of Oakland to America's Team out of Dallas. From Bill Walsh and the 49ers' West Coast Offense to the Joe Gibbs Redskins. From the Bears' 46 Defense to the Cowboys' Triplets. From John Elway concluding his Hall of Fame career with not one, but two championship finales to Tom Brady beginning his future Hall of Fame career at age 24 with his first title.

Add in Doug Williams becoming the first African-American quarterback to take the crown with Washington in 1988, and Tony Dungy as the first African-American coach to win it in 2007—beating another black coach, his friend and former assistant Lovie Smith.

All helped form the legacy of the Super Bowl.

SHORT LIST

The Top Super Bowl Winning Franchises through 2016

Pittsburgh (6), San Francisco (5), Dallas (5), New England (4), New York Giants (4), Green Bay (4), Los Angeles–Oakland (3), Washington (3), Denver (3).

Along the way, America has watched with unparalleled interest. TV ratings aren't the only way to measure the Super Bowl's draw and impact, but they are an effective way. Consider that every year, the game is the most-watched event on the tube, with nothing else really close.

Super Bowl XLIX, New England's last-second win over Seattle, drew a 47.5 rating and a 71 share. That means more than 114 million people watched, with estimates of more than 120 million seeing the final 10 minutes.

"Right now the NFL and the Super Bowl are defying media gravity," Mark Lazarus, NBC Sports Group chairman, told The Associated Press.

NBC also offered live streaming of the game to computers and tablets, with an average of 800,000 people watching per minute.

Additionally, the Super Bowl is the consummate event for social media. Facebook had about 65 million people converse about the 2015 game on the site; there were some 265 million individual posts, comments, or likes, according to Facebook. And Twitter estimated 28.4 million tweets posted between kickoff and 30 minutes after the game's conclusion.

How many of those viewers had money on the game? Plenty.

Listen to Jay Kornegay, who runs the sports book at LVH in Las Vegas and offers the usual wagers (point spreads, over-and-under totals, score by quarters) and the outrageous (who will win the coin toss; how long the rendition of the national anthem by whichever superstar singer is chosen will last).

"It's not just an amenity anymore; it's not just icing on the cake, it's part of the meal," Kornegay told the *St. Louis Post-Dispatch*. "We've seen crowds like we've never seen before."

And they want to bet on anything and everything.

"Some of them made bets just to take the ticket home with them," Jimmy Vaccaro of South Point sports book told Bleacher Report, "To show their other friends . . . this is the crazy stuff I was betting on."

Vaccaro recalls the 1986 game between the Bears, with perhaps the most powerful defense in history—Monsters of the Midway indeed—and the Patriots. But what he remembers is not how Chicago manhandled New England's offense, but something Bears coach Mike Ditka did on offense that changed Super Bowl betting forever.

Ditka called for a handoff to defensive tackle William "The Refrigerator" Perry, not future Hall of Fame running back Walter Payton, when Chicago was at the New England 1. Because Perry had been used in such a role during the season, oddsmakers had placed a 40-to-1 line on him scoring in the big game. Touchdown.

"That was the prop that put everybody on the map," Vaccaro said. "We lost $40,000 on one bet and the guy across the street blew so much he wanted to go upstairs and jump off the roof."

Only in the Super Bowl.

Also only in the Super Bowl come TV commercials designed for the massive audience and unveiled at various points of the game—at a price tag now approaching $5 million for 30 seconds. Commercials in the first Super Bowl cost $42,000. So do the math: The cost of one second of air time now would have gotten advertisers three full commercials in 1967.

The commercials draw so much attention that *USA Today* devotes separate coverage to them, including Ad Meter rating the winners and losers. Ads involving animals, children, and technology are usually considered the most successful. The worst? Try anything depressing or incomprehensible—of which there have been many.

Always a huge part of the show is, well, the show. No, not what the guys in helmets and pads are putting on, but the halftime performances (see Game Changer 50), which last twice as long as the usual 13 minutes of break during regular-season and playoff games. Speculation on who will have the "honor" of entertaining at halftime tends to begin about a week after the previous Super Bowl. The acts, who get roughly 12 minutes to perform, have ranged from marching bands at the first five games—the University of Arizona and Grambling State were at the initial Super Bowl—to Up With People (look it up!) to Diana Ross, Michael Jackson, Paul McCartney, the Rolling Stones, Bruce Springsteen, and Madonna.

Usually, those shows go smoothly, though the NFL and game broadcaster CBS were aghast when Justin Timberlake revealed Janet Jackson's breast to the audience in Houston and millions watching on TV in the infamous "wardrobe malfunction" in 2004.

That's what the Super Bowl has become, an event with no boundaries.

Then again, that's what the Super Bowl has become, an event with no boundaries other than those on the field.

But considering all of the tangential attachments, defining the Super Bowl as nothing more than the championship game of pro football is a colossal understatement. And nothing about the Super Bowl is understated anymore.

Pete Rozelle
Two Decades in Charge of Major Change

NO. 3

Pro football might have become America's premier sport without Pete Rozelle's leadership. But it simply would have taken years, maybe decades longer to reach that level.

In the 1930s and 40s, the NFL took a backseat to baseball, boxing, and, in some years, horse racing. It wasn't even the most popular form of football in this country—the college game was.

Not a lot had changed in the 1950s under Bert Bell. Then Alvin "Pete" Rozelle became something of a compromise commissioner after Bell passed away. And everything changed.

Rozelle played basketball and tennis in high school, then entered the Navy, serving in the Pacific from 1944 to 1946. He returned to attend a junior college in his hometown of Compton, California, and got a part-time job working in the Rams' publicity department; the team had just moved from Cleveland to Los Angeles.

Rozelle then attended the University of San Francisco and took on the role of publicity director for the athletics program. In 1950, following graduation, he became the school's assistant athletic director. In 1952 he became the Rams PR man.

So his background wasn't exactly administrative. It certainly wasn't in business or the legal world. But he was a rising star within the league and became the Rams' general manager in 1957. Still, his credentials for becoming the league's boss didn't seem quite so established.

NFL owners met for more than a week and eventually 23 ballots were cast.

"The meetings went on maybe 10 days—day and night sessions—and an impasse developed," Rozelle said. "As I recall, seven clubs were supporting Marshall Leahy, who was an attorney for the San Francisco 49ers, and then you had four other clubs who supported several other people: judges, team people, all sorts of others."

Three of the most influential owners eventually suggested and backed Rozelle: Wellington Mara of the New York Giants, Dan Reeves of the Rams, and Paul Brown of the Cleveland Browns. Early on in the process, the 33-year-old Rozelle didn't even know he was a candidate. Then, he was the new commissioner.

Pete Rozelle (left) and George Halas at the dedication ceremony of the George S. Halas, Jr. Sports Center

AUDIBLE

On the Commish

"I firmly believe that when the final history of the National Football League is written, the all-time hero of the NFL, the man who contributed the most to changing America's Sunday afternoon watching habits, is Pete Rozelle." —*Edwin Pope, Miami Herald*

"I was totally shocked," he said, "because I was so young and because they'd considered so many other people who had so much more experience in football than I."

Rozelle immediately warmed to the task.

He moved the league offices from Bell's home city of Philadelphia to midtown Manhattan, recognizing that to become a major player in the media and sponsorship world, the NFL had to be in the media and sponsorship capital of the world.

The next step was perhaps the most significant in Rozelle's two decades in charge: signing a network television deal. He got that done with CBS for $600,000 for the entire 1960 season—hardly a landmark number at that time, but the beginning of football's meteoric rise in TV sports rights, the beginning of pro football's explosion. Within two years, the fees had increased to $4.65 million. By his retirement in 1989, that number was more than a billion dollars.

Rozelle also quickly realized the NFL needed two ingredients as a cornerstone of its growth: an antitrust exemption from Congress, and revenue sharing. He successfully lobbied for the limited antitrust exemption in 1961, something that would clear the way for the AFL-NFL merger in 1966, and many other major initiatives the league has undertaken.

Revenue sharing of TV money was more dicey.

Baseball, still America's pastime, didn't have it, but Rozelle wisely recognized that without it, such franchises as the Packers and Steelers in smaller markets—indeed, Green Bay remains the smallest of pro sports markets—wouldn't survive.

"Pete wasn't just looking out for the smaller cities, he was looking out for everyone," Mara said. "He understood that having everyone on an equal playing field, if you will, meant everyone could compete. That wasn't quite true with the other [sports]."

Persuading Papa Bear George Halas, Washington's George Preston Marshall, and some of the other hard-liners of the benefits of revenue sharing wasn't so easy. Rozelle basically was asking some of the richest and most profitable franchise owners to look down the road—far down the road—to long-term stability. That he got it done relatively painlessly was a tribute to Rozelle's persuasiveness, foresight, and power.

"What Pete Rozelle did with television receipts," Vince Lombardi said, "probably saved football in Green Bay."

Next up was growing the membership, and Rozelle was ahead of the game there, too. In 1960, the Cowboys came to Dallas for a $1 million expansion fee. The next year, the Vikings came to life in Minnesota for the same fee. Not long after, Atlanta and New Orleans came aboard for $8.5 million each. When he was done, he'd taken the NFL team roster from 12 teams worth perhaps $1 million each to 28 with a total value of more than $100 million.

There was plenty of intrigue to go along with the Saints joining the NFL, and Rozelle was at the heart of that, too.

With the AFL-NFL war ongoing, Rozelle needed hefty congressional support to get a merger approved without violating any antitrust acts. Louisiana Democrat Hale Boggs had enough influence within Congress to help the NFL, but at a price: a franchise for New Orleans. The league knew that a merger would bring in some new territories, but Bayou Country was not necessarily one of them.

To become a major player in the media and sponsorship world, the NFL had to be in the media and sponsorship capital of the world.

"He was majority whip and Russell Long was majority whip of the Senate. If they couldn't do it, who could?" ABC journalist Cokie Roberts, Boggs's daughter, told the *New York Times*.

Boggs virtually guaranteed approval of the merger, which would be included in an anti-inflation bill, with the price being an NFL team in the Big Easy. Rozelle demurred at first, saying he had to put it before the owners.

When Boggs countered with a suggestion that any legislative vote could be "put off for a while," Rozelle swallowed hard. He needed clear sailing on combining the AFL with the NFL. "You'll have your team," he assured Boggs.

Rozelle didn't have clear sailing in all facets of the job early on. Two of his toughest decisions came in 1963, one of which he regretted for the remainder of his life.

An investigation revealed that two of the league's biggest stars, Packers running back Paul Hornung and Lions defensive tackle Alex Karras, had bet on their own teams. The NFL had already established its strong opposition to gambling—some say hypocritically so because of how much interest all the betting on games brings to the sport—and Rozelle suspended each of them for the '63 season.

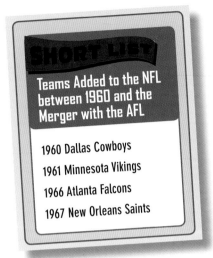

SHORT LIST

Teams Added to the NFL between 1960 and the Merger with the AFL

1960 Dallas Cowboys

1961 Minnesota Vikings

1966 Atlanta Falcons

1967 New Orleans Saints

"I thought about it at length," Rozelle told *Sports Illustrated*. "The maximum penalty for a player would be suspension for life. That would be for failure to report a bribe attempt or for trying to shave points.

"This sport has grown so quickly and gained so much of the approval of the American public that the only way it can be hurt is through gambling. . . .

"I also took into account that the violations of Hornung and Karras were continuing, not casual. They were continuing, flagrant, and increasing. Both players had been informed over and over of the league rule on gambling; the rule is posted in every clubhouse in the league, as well. Yet they continued to gamble. I could only exact from them the most severe penalty short of banishment for life."

Both returned the next year, and Hornung eventually made the Pro Football Hall of Fame.

On November 22, President John F. Kennedy was assassinated in Dallas. While the AFL immediately called off its games scheduled for that weekend, Rozelle wavered. He consulted with Pierre Salinger, a friend from college and JFK's press secretary. Salinger encouraged Rozelle to have the games played.

"It has been traditional in sports for athletes to perform in times of great personal tragedy," Rozelle said while announcing the NFL would play that Sunday. "Football was Mr. Kennedy's game. He thrived on competition."

In later years, Rozelle admitted it was "the worst decision I ever made."

Once he saw through the merger in 1966 that would be finalized in 1970, Rozelle set about further establishing his sport's TV presence, and figuring out the dynamics for a championship game between the formerly warring and now supposedly friendly leagues.

First on his rapidly filling plate was convincing NFL owners—and not just a few, as with revenue sharing, but all of them—that an AFL-NFL championship game was a must.

"To fully conclude the merger, we needed one championship team," Rozelle said. "That meant a championship game, AFL versus NFL."

While that game didn't become known as the Super Bowl until the third edition in 1969, it came together as quickly as Rozelle had been urging.

A more offbeat idea, which Rozelle championed for several years before it came to fruition in 1970, was a weekly prime-time NFL game.

The problem was neither NBC nor CBS, the network partners of the AFL and NFL, respectively, had any interest in interrupting their prime-time lineups. Sports didn't quite sell back then the way it would in the next few decades. The NFL's programming draw certainly paled in comparison to today, when night games are a guaranteed ratings (and advertising revenue) bonanza.

But Rozelle found a willing partner in ABC, where Roone Arledge was about to become the most innovative producer in television. In Week 1 of the 1970 season, the Jets and Browns met in prime time. It was the beginning of the longest-running sports TV series, still going strong (on ESPN) today.

TV executives had learned that Rozelle could be as forceful as he needed to be, but that he understood the needs of the networks, too.

"Pete would be so reserved and speak in such a low voice you could hardly hear him," former CBS executive Neil Pilson said. "[Browns owner] Art Modell would jump up and down, turn colors and say the teams were suffering.

"With Pete, there was no effort to play networks against each other, but he was prepared to do it if you didn't step up. He assured us that he was giving the other networks just as hard a time."

Rozelle was inducted into the Pro Football Hall of Fame in a distinguished class that also included Roger Staubach, Joe Namath, and, well, O. J. Simpson.

Harder times would come to the NFL even as Rozelle kept filling teams' coffers with loot, and the game's popularity skyrocketed. Labor issues wore down Rozelle, who in 1974 had been given a 10-year contract extension. Feuds with Raiders owner Al Davis, who was commissioner of the AFL during the merger and longed for Rozelle's job, also left a sour taste.

But on August 3, 1985, Rozelle was inducted into the Pro Football Hall of Fame in a distinguished class that also included Roger Staubach, Joe Namath, and, well, O. J. Simpson.

Rozelle got a kick out of entering the hall with Broadway Joe, the architect of the biggest upset in Super Bowl history.

"I didn't say it at the time, I kept a dour face for our old employees in the NFL," Rozelle told the *New York Times*. "But I felt the Jets' victory was a very significant day in the history of the NFL—it strengthened us as a league."

In 1999, three years after he died of brain cancer, the *Sporting News* selected Rozelle as the 20th century's most powerful sportsman.

"He'll forever be remembered as the standard by which all sports executives are judged," Mara said.

Black Breakthrough

Motley, Washington, Strode, and Willis Come to Play in 1946

Kenny Washington was waiting for a phone call.

The star running back of the UCLA Bruins was expecting to hear from George Halas, owner of the Chicago Bears. Halas had promised Washington he would be in touch following the 1940 College All-Star Game in Chicago's Soldier Field, where Washington had capped a glorious college career by scoring a touchdown.

Halas had been impressed. So much so that he had asked Washington to stick around Chicago so he could try to find a roster spot for him on the Bears. So Washington waited. One day passed. Then another. Finally, after a week, Halas called and told Washington, sorry, he couldn't use him.

Washington, you see, was black.

From 1934 to 1945, the NFL had an unwritten rule against using black players. Though Washington had an incredible college career, he along with other outstanding African Americans was blacklisted in the NFL.

Blacks had played in the NFL before 1934, but for the next 12 years the league would be segregated, as owners simply followed baseball's lead and ignored minority players.

A bitter disappointment for the greatest football player that nobody remembers.

As one of the top running backs of his day, Washington's feats at UCLA were legendary. He scored 19 career touchdowns and set five records for the Bruins, including total offense (3,206 yards) and interceptions (six).

But numbers alone didn't tell Washington's whole story. Playing in the same backfield as Jackie Robinson (yes, *that* Jackie Robinson, the man who broke baseball's color line with the Brooklyn Dodgers in 1947), Washington was an incomparable college football player.

Kenny Washington was among the first African Americans to play at UCLA and in the NFL.

And Washington would eventually break the football color line in 1946 through a twist of fate.

Washington's versatility was amazing, and it didn't matter if he was playing offense or defense. Whether passing or punting, blocking, tackling, pass defending, or running as an outside/inside ball carrier, Washington was simply superb.

Robinson said that Washington was the best football player he had ever seen. In a 1962 *Sports Illustrated* story, "The Best College Player of All Time," Washington was ranked with other all-time greats.

Washington had an unusually strong arm, throwing prodigious passes that often traveled long distances during a time when deep passing was not common. In one UPI account of a game in 1939, one of Washington's passes traveled 76 yards in the air. That season Washington finished sixth in Heisman Trophy balloting.

At the time, segregation was rampant in America. It was an all-white world in each of the major professional sports: baseball, football, basketball, and hockey.

With its fragmented history regarding African-American players, professional football got a head start on the other sports in 1904. That year a black player, Charles Follis, was paid to play for the Shelby (Ohio) Athletic Club. In 1920, Fritz Pollard was the first great black football star, playing for the Akron Pros in a league that was the forerunner of the NFL.

From 1920, the league's first season, to 1934, a total of 13 black players appeared in the NFL, according to a report by the Pro Football Research Association (PFRA).

College football and baseball were far more popular than professional football at this time. While pro football was trying to establish itself in the American consciousness, Kenny Washington was developing his talents in football and baseball in Lincoln Heights, California. He was raised mostly by a grandmother, and an uncle who became the first black lieutenant in the Los Angeles Police Department.

From 1920, the league's first season, to 1934, a total of 13 black players appeared in the NFL.

In 1936, Washington enrolled at UCLA. He met Woody Strode, another black teammate, when they were both freshmen. Jackie Robinson came to the Los Angeles school as a junior in 1939. At one point Washington and Robinson played in the same backfield, while Strode starred at the end position.

The three became wildly popular. Washington and Robinson were supreme athletes, both playing baseball as well as football for the Bruins.

It was for his football skills that Washington would be most remembered at UCLA. In his last year, the 6-foot-1, 195-pound Washington earned All-America honors.

On Playing College Baseball with Jackie Robinson

"Next to me, Jackie was the best competitor I ever saw. But when he became a baseball star, it kind of shook me. I out-hit him by at least 200 points at UCLA." —*Kenny Washington*

AUDIBLE

Washington and Robinson were a great one-two punch in the Bruins' backfield, with Robinson not only running but also catching his share of Washington's passes.

Facing all-white teams, Washington was a target for bigots. Name calling was frequent. In more than one game, opponents would shove Washington's face into the lime used to line the field. Strode and fellow Bruins would later settle the score.

But Washington never retaliated.

"If Kenny knocked a guy down, he'd pick him up after the play was over," Strode said.

Upon graduation in 1940, Washington joined the Hollywood Bears, a semipro team in the Pacific Coast League that was open to black players. He later played for the San Francisco Clippers of the AFL. His salary in the semipro leagues from 1940 to 1945 ranged from $50 to $100 a game, substantially less than players were making in the NFL.

In 1946, Washington finally got his chance to play in the NFL, but it took some enterprising maneuvering to finally break the color line (for the second time).

With the war over, times were changing. A large influx of blacks attracted by jobs in the defense industries now lived in Southern California. President Franklin Delano Roosevelt had outlawed segregation in the defense industry, but the NFL was still segregated. Black servicemen came home with new expectations, but policies still barred them from many areas that were kept segregated.

The NFL was about to get a jolt. It happened when owner Dan Reeves of the Cleveland Rams decided to move his team to Southern California from Cleveland in 1946. Reeves felt that the untapped West Coast would present golden opportunities for his team, not to mention the league itself.

Reeves wanted to lease the Los Angeles Coliseum. But there was a roadblock. Three black newspaper sportswriters objected. Halley Harving, Herman Hill, and Abie Robinson felt that an all-white team should not be playing in a publicly owned facility. They got the support of the Los Angeles Commission and the commissioner, Leonard Roach.

"The Coliseum people warned the Rams if they practiced discrimination, they couldn't use the stadium," said Washington. They insisted that Washington be given a tryout as part of the arrangement for the home field. No problem. Washington made the team.

Reeves was fine with this arrangement. Despite vigorous objections by NFL owners, in March 1946 Reeves signed the 28-year-old Washington. He had had five knee operations during his semipro days, yet Washington managed to compete.

It would take a while for the owners to change their way of thinking.

"When those NFL people began thinking about all those seats and the money they could make filling them up, they decided my kind wasn't so bad after all," Washington later said.

Shortly after, the LA Rams brought in Woodrow Wilson "Woody" Strode. Yes, the same black teammate from Washington's years at UCLA. He became the second black player to sign with an NFL team since 1933.

Washington clearly wasn't the same player who had dazzled opponents in his collegiate days. In 1939 while playing tailback and safety at UCLA, he missed only 20 minutes of a possible 600, an amazing feat of endurance. The years, from his days at UCLA through several seasons of semipro ball, had taken their toll. But there were flashes of his old greatness.

In a 1947 game against the Chicago Cardinals, Washington raced 92 yards from scrimmage for a touchdown. While there weren't many other spectacular runs like that, Washington was effective. In three years with the Rams, he averaged 6-plus yards a carry and 859 yards total. He suffered many unpenalized late hits.

The addition of Strode, his teammate at UCLA, didn't ease the situation. After three years in the NFL, Washington retired from professional football, the shell of a once-great player.

Today, black players make up nearly 70 percent of the NFL.

Rams fans certainly appreciated Washington, 80,000 of them coming out in the Coliseum to pay him tribute in 1948.

Strode, meanwhile, lasted only one year in the NFL and two more in the Canadian Football League before quitting to start a lucrative career in the movies. He worked with some of Hollywood's top actors, including Burt Lancaster, Kirk Douglas, and John Wayne. It was said that Strode worked in more Hollywood films than most black actors at the time.

Soon after Washington and Strode were signed, the All-America Conference put a team in Cleveland coached by Paul Brown. Brown was familiar with two black players, Marion Motley and Bill Willis, and his all-white team was about to change. He was looking for talent, white or black. He had coached Willis at Ohio State and Motley at one of the wartime powerhouses, Great Lakes Naval Training Center in Illinois. So the fall after Washington signed, Willis and Motley were on the Cleveland Browns.

Motley, a 6-foot-1, 240-pound fullback, inadvertently helped create two of pro football's iconic plays—the draw play and the screen pass.

On pass plays, Motley would stay in the backfield and block for quarterback Otto Graham. The draw play developed when Graham escaped a hard rush with a late handoff to Motley.

The screen play happened when a tackler came loose and Graham flipped the ball to his fullback, who turned upfield. In the words of some NFL defenders, the result was "terrifying."

"If you didn't stop him at the line of scrimmage," said defensive tackle Art Donovan, "you were in trouble."

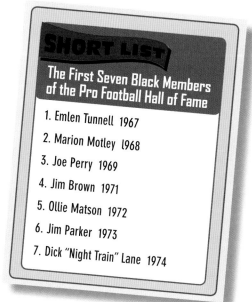

SHORT LIST

The First Seven Black Members of the Pro Football Hall of Fame

1. Emlen Tunnell 1967
2. Marion Motley 1968
3. Joe Perry 1969
4. Jim Brown 1971
5. Ollie Matson 1972
6. Jim Parker 1973
7. Dick "Night Train" Lane 1974

Motley believed that he was brought into the Browns' camp simply because the coaches needed a black roommate for Willis. According to Brown, this was untrue: He had planned all along to bring Motley to camp.

The 6-foot-1, 210-pound Willis would soon be regarded as one of the quickest linemen in the league. In practice his reactions were so quick that he confused teammates with moves that left them fumbling and stepping on each other's feet. They complained that Willis had to be cheating on the snap. To answer his players' complaints, Brown got down on his hands and knees and peered through the line to watch the action. Brown concluded that Willis was not offside, but just moved with the ball at a quicker pace than the other linemen.

Motley and Willis had Hall of Fame careers. Even though they were mistreated by white players, they kept their tempers in check, as dictated by Paul Brown. They faced adversity both on and off the field, but adhered to Brown's rules not to retaliate.

Today, black players make up nearly 70 percent of the NFL, which has become the most popular sport in America. They follow in the large footsteps of men whose names few know.

Kenny Washington is one of them, a name we should all remember. Along with Woody Strode, Bill Willis, and Marion Motley.

Making Football "Safe"

Though known as a "Rough Rider" who spoke softly and carried a big stick, even this was too much for Teddy Roosevelt.

The number of deaths and serious injuries in college football in 1905 was particularly disturbing to the president and the nation.

The sport had been under heavy scrutiny for years by the press, physicians, and college administrators. The '05 season brought more attention to the crises. According to newspaper reports, 18 college players had died and 159 were seriously injured that year. Spinal cord injuries, gouged eyes, crushed skulls, and broken bones were commonplace in the sport. A bloody newspaper photo of an injured player increased the public clamor for a ban or reform.

NO. **1**

Roosevelt, whose own son played for Harvard and was injured, wasn't about to join those who wanted to ban the sport. He loved football too much.

Even back in 1893, Roosevelt had published an article in defense of the sport.

Roosevelt wrote that risk was inherent in the sport, but rather than kill it, reform in football was needed to "minimize" its dangers. But now he was seriously concerned about where the game was heading.

Throughout his political career, Roosevelt had made a name for himself as a reformer, and he was proud of it. He had also been an explorer, naturalist, and author. He had made his reputation as a soldier who famously charged up San Juan Hill leading American troops in the Spanish-American War.

Now he was serving as the 26th president of the United States. In the country's highest office, Roosevelt had a Wild West persona that underscored his masculinity. And he was determined to clean up football before he left office.

Roosevelt brought together the football powers of his time to reform the game.

On the Thought of Abolishing Football

"It is mere unmanly folly to try to do away with the sport because the risk exists." —*future president Theodore Roosevelt, 1893*

AUDIBLE

It wasn't until 1905, however, that Roosevelt met the problem head-on. Five universities announced they were dropping their football programs unless there were reforms. Something had to be done to protect the players from injury; eliminate scandals involving eligibility and gambling; clarify rules; persuade the public that the sport was a worthwhile pursuit; and deter those that wished to end football altogether.

It was first down and a long way to go for college football.

The president summoned coaches from Harvard, Yale, and Princeton, the elite football colleges from the Ivy League, to the White House. Roosevelt's mandate: develop a game plan to make football safer.

The coaches signed a safety pledge. Later that month, 62 schools committed to overhaul the game. They formed a rules committee under the name of the Intercollegiate Athletic Association (IAA). It became the foundation for the National Collegiate Athletic Association (NCAA). This governing body was seen as a very positive development, creating an entity to enforce the rules changes and increase penalties for "unnecessary roughness."

History was about to be made.

The first college football game in America had been played in 1869 between Rutgers and Princeton. And 37 years later, the face of the game was about to completely change. No longer would only brute strength be required to move the ball. On January 12, 1906, the group legalized the forward pass. The idea was to spread the players apart and decrease the amount of contact.

There were other rules changes, such as altering yardage for a first down from 5 to 10 (in three downs) and establishing a neutral zone on the line of scrimmage. The four-down concept would come into play later, in 1912.

Of all the rules, the forward pass was the most controversial. It was promoted vigorously by John Heisman, whose name would become legendary with the Heisman Trophy signifying the top college football player in America.

Coach Walter Camp was familiar with dangerous collisions, having engineered the "flying wedge" at Yale. The "wedge," or "V-Wedge," as it was known, sent the ball carrier behind a wall of blockers at the weakest part of the opponent's defensive line. The mass of bodies would crash into each other. Rarely were penalties called.

Coach Walter Camp was familiar with dangerous collisions, having engineered the "flying wedge" at Yale.

"What a grand play!" the *New York Times* marveled at one point. "A half-ton of bone and muscle coming into collision with a man weighing 160 or 170 pounds."

Because of its spectacular violence, the Wedge was soon banned from the game.

Yet not everybody agreed with the move away from flying wedges toward spiraling footballs.

Camp believed the players would be facing more danger. The pass would only make matters worse, he reasoned, with men streaking downfield and crashing into each other with more opportunities for injury.

When the forward pass was legalized, it was thought it would have a major impact on the game. Instead, it was largely ignored. Few coaches actually saw the potential, only the disadvantages. Among the new rules, a pass could not be caught more than 20 yards from the line of scrimmage. If the pass was incomplete on the first or second down, the offensive team would be charged with a 15-yard penalty from the spot of the pass. If the receiver failed to get 5 yards with the pass, it led to an automatic change of possession.

Thankfully, some—like Eddie Cochems—did see the potential.

Cochems was in his first year as coach of the St. Louis University (SLU) football team. And like almost every coach in America, Cochems was caught up in digesting the new rules.

"I think that the pass will develop many beautiful, spectacular plays before the season closes," he said.

And Cochems' SLU team was the one to produce them.

He became fascinated by the so-called "blimp ball" that looked like a watermelon. He determined it was made for kicking or to be carried under the arm while running—not for passing. However, if the fingers were held a certain way on the laces, the potential for success became greater.

Cochems believed college football was destined to spread its wings with aerial attacks. During the summer of 1906, he convinced SLU officials to send him and 16 men to a Jesuit sanctuary in Lake Beulah, Wisconsin, for "the sole purpose of studying and developing the pass," Cochems wrote to the *St. Louis Post-Dispatch* in 1940. By the time the players returned home, they were fully prepared to unveil their powerful new weapon.

"We were loaded with a sort of atomic football bomb that astounded and wrecked all opposition," said SLU star Frank Acker.

SLU opened its season with an exhibition game on September 5, 1906, with Carroll College. The little school from Waukesha, Wisconsin, gave SLU a test at the start. The teams were locked in a scoreless tie when Cochems decided to unleash his new weapon.

Bradbury Robinson, the SLU quarterback, had practiced the forward pass until he became an expert at gaining long distances. Now it was time to show his stuff.

His first attempt was incomplete. According to the rules, the ball was turned over to Carroll College.

But on his next possession came the biggest surprise to everyone, especially the Carroll College defense. Robinson threw a pass to Jack Schneider covering 20 yards. This time the receiver held on. Touchdown!

It was reportedly the first legal pass in college football after the new rules were adopted.

SLU beat Carroll 22–0 and Cochems was largely regarded as the father of the forward pass.

Seven years later, Notre Dame's Knute Rockne would help develop the pass to an even higher level.

An official at the Notre Dame–Army game of 1913 wrote that, "he knew such play was possible under the new existing rules, but he had never seen the forward pass developed to such a state of perfection."

It all started when Army was looking to add an easy game to its schedule in 1913. A meeting was arranged with Notre Dame. No one in the East knew anything about the Irish, and Army figured to have little trouble with this small college from the Midwest.

At the time, eastern teams looked down on teams in the Midwest. The East boasted the best football in the country, particularly the Ivy League, which was where the sport began.

The game was played at West Point, another factor in Army's favor. If they were giving odds in Las Vegas, the Notre Dame–Army game would have been taken off the betting board.

The summer before the game, Rockne and his roommate, Gus Dorais, worked on plays to surprise the Army defense. Dorais, the quarterback, and Rockne, the receiver, concentrated on a better way to throw and catch the ball. A rule change that became effective that fall had removed all restrictions on the length of a legal forward pass.

THE TWELFTH PLAYER IN EVERY FOOTBALL GAME.

From Joseph Pulitzer's *New York World*. An 1897 cartoon depicting "death" as the twelfth man on the field.

Game time: Notre Dame vs. Army, November 1, 1913, with 3,000 in attendance at West Point. The opening series of plays portended trouble for the Irish. Dorais fumbled and Army recovered on the Notre Dame 27 yard line. The Irish stiffened, holding Army to one yard on three plays. It gave the Black Knights a good indication of what they were in for that afternoon.

"Let's open up," Dorais said in the huddle.

The Irish did, as Dorais completed an 11-yard pass to Rockne.

"It was amusing to see the Army boys huddle after a first, snappy 11-yard pass had been completed for a first down," Rockne once recalled. "Their guards and tackles went tumbling into us to stop the bucks and plunges. Instead, Dorais stepped neatly back and flicked the ball to an uncovered end or halfback. Our attack had been well rehearsed."

Indeed. And no one ever expected Dorais's long-distance passes, some of which traveled as far as 40 yards. Also unheard of was the number of passes thrown that day by the Notre Dame quarterback: 17. He completed 14 for 243 yards.

At the end of a 35–13 Notre Dame victory, the *New York Times* reported: "The Westerners flashed the most sensational football ever seen in the East."

The movie *Knute Rockne, All-American*, starring Ronald Reagan as the Gipper, kept alive a myth. The movie had portrayed Rockne as the inventor of the forward pass. Rockne said that was far from the truth.

"The press and football public hailed this new game, and Notre Dame received credit as the originator of a style of play that we had simply systematized," Rockne said.

A month after SLU beat Carroll, Wesleyan scored a touchdown using the forward pass against Yale, setting up a controversy over who threw the first pass. SLU claimed the distinction because its pass came first. But supporters for Wesleyan noted that the SLU-Carroll game was merely an exhibition.

While not claiming to have "invented" the forward pass, Notre Dame used it as the team's vehicle to national prominence.

By 1910 the IAA had become the NCAA. A few years later, the forward pass was becoming more popular, though none had perfected it as well as Rockne. Football was becoming less brutal, though there were still injuries and deaths.

But now there was an organization overseeing the sport.

As the NCAA came of age, it became more powerful and intrusive. Rules kept changing to keep up with the times. The NCAA became a powerful and dominant organization in college sports. With money and power came controversy and criticism.

Walter Byers was the first executive director of the NCAA. He successfully led the organization into prominence from 1951 to 1987 and became one of sports' most powerful figures. Today the NCAA supervises 90 sports, has more than 1,100 member colleges, and its revenue approaches $1 billion, mostly thanks to the foundation established by Byers. Yet, after his retirement, he became one of the organization's biggest critics.

The NCAA oversees all areas of college sports: eligibility, championships, financial aid restrictions, scholarships, sports divisions, and television rights, among others. The Bowl

Championship Series (BCS) was created to determine a college champion in football, and in 2015, they played the inaugural College Football Playoff National Championship, with a four-team bracket system determining the national champion.

Much of the NCAA's disciplinary powers involve recruiting violations, small and large. In cases of extreme rules violations, the NCAA has the power to impose a "death penalty" by banning a school from a particular sport for two years. Massive NCAA rules violations caused Southern Methodist University to receive the "death penalty" in 1985; once a football power, the school has yet to recover fully on the field.

> **Much of the NCAA's disciplinary powers involve recruiting violations, small and large. In cases of extreme rules violations, the NCAA has the power to impose a "death penalty."**

In the infamous Penn State scandal involving Jerry Sandusky and Joe Paterno, the NCAA "death penalty" was considered. Instead, the NCAA penalized Penn State by taking away a substantial number of Paterno's victories, reducing the number of scholarships, and excluding the Nittany Lions from postseason play for four years. In addition, Penn State was fined $60 million.

This created lots of debate, many feeling that the investigation was not thorough and the penalties too harsh. Football nation was in turmoil over the incident, which stimulated discussion worldwide.

Many thought Paterno was convicted by the NCAA without trial. Responding to legal action, the NCAA finally returned Paterno's victories, some of the scholarships, and made the Nittany Lions bowl eligible once more.

Other NCAA rules stimulate strong feelings pro and con.

Take the concept of the "student athlete." The NCAA has long held that no compensation shall be given to the student athlete. With television revenues growing and universities profiting from the play of these young men and women, many feel the time has come for compensation. The NCAA argues it would undermine the student athletes' status as amateurs. The discussion is ongoing, with strong supporters on both sides.

One has to wonder what Theodore Roosevelt would think of all of this. The drive to save football was certainly successful, but many of the safety concerns of long ago remain today with bigger, faster and more powerful athletes engaged in one of the most violent of sports.

The discussion continues.

Point Spreads and Fantasy Football

Is Gambling the Real Reason Football Is America's Sporting Obsession?

NO. 6

American sports fans are obsessed with the gridiron. "Fan" is a shortened version of fanatic, after all.

The violence of the game has its attraction for many. The way the NFL and the colleges market the sport, the way TV goes overboard in constantly discussing it, even when there won't be a kickoff for months, all help boost football beyond baseball, basketball, and anything else involving athletics in America.

Oh yeah, there's also a little bit of interest from gamblers and fantasy participants. Just a little.

In 2014, bookmakers in Las Vegas, where wagering on sporting events is legal, took in $1.8 billion in bets on NFL and college football games. They made $114 million in profit, setting records for money wagered and money lost on football.

That's just one segment of the betting industry in one location, albeit the mecca of sports wagering. Extrapolate those numbers to include office pools and betting sheets; lottery games based on football; and, since the turn of the century, fantasy leagues, including the newest lucrative choices, daily fantasy options. Fantasy football alone involved more than $20 billion in expenditures by its participants in 2014.

Other sports have betting lines and fantasy teams. Nothing touches football.

A Las Vegas sportsbook

On Hanging Up One's Fantasy Spikes

"They've surveyed fantasy sports players and asked, 'When do you expect to quit?' And the average response is, 'Never.'"
—*Nigel Eccles, chief executive officer and co-founder of FanDuel*

AUDIBLE

So when the NFL challenges the legality of various states instituting sports gambling, just remember that without all of those dollars being put down on the Packers or Seahawks or whomever, the league isn't a $10-plus billion entity headed for a much higher stratosphere.

One person who probably belongs in a variety of football halls of fame—and certainly in the oddsmakers' and bettors' shrines—is Charles McNeil. Don't bother looking up his stats as an athlete, because he never contributed on the field. Instead, McNeil changed the game by inventing the point spread. A graduate of the University of Chicago, McNeil went into banking. He also was a frequent bettor on several sports and a good oddsmaker. He recognized the possibility for enticing more wagering by getting away from the normal odds associated with straight bets.

So McNeil came up with what he termed "wholesale odds," or giving the underdog team a certain number of points. Bet on the favorite, you'd have to lay those points.

The point spread.

The idea took off, not only in Chicago, where McNeil ran his parlors, but nationwide. "Money, guts, and brains," he said. "If you don't have one, you're dead. I've got all three." As Jimmy Vaccaro, one of Las Vegas's most influential bookmakers, said of McNeil: "The guy was way ahead of his time. A remarkable man from everything I have found out about him. An absolute genius."

As the point spread evolved through the years, so did more exotic bets—just like in horse racing, where tracks began offering more than straight wagers on the outcome of a race, or daily doubles. Exactas, perfectas, quinellas.

In football, parlays became popular: string together a bunch of victories against the spread and collect big-time. Bookmakers loved that idea; it's difficult enough to hit one game while laying or getting points. More than one? Show me the money, the bookies said.

"I used to pull customers aside and tell them that parlay cards pay my salary and for the lights in the casino," sports book director and handicapper Raphael Esparza told The Associated Press. "If you're going to live and die on betting parlays the whole season, I'll mortgage my house against your house."

He'd probably do the same for all of those bizarre bets that accompany the Super Bowl: length of the national anthem; who wins the coin toss and what decision they'll make; first player to lose yardage or be penalized.

A cottage industry has been created as part of the betting frenzy: touts who will give you "guaranteed winners and money makers" against the spread. For a price, of course.

Professional handicapper Joe Falchetti explained the phenomenon—and why the buyer must beware.

"A tout's bread and butter is the NFL season and these guys know it," he wrote on Foot ballbetting.net. "They actively promote themselves (and their 'expert' handicapping picks) in the preseason, throughout the season, up until the Super Bowl. Many advertise on the radio, through internet sites and in magazines. They say they are professionals and they tell you that they are going to help you win big all season long, but the only catch is that you have to pay for their advice. If you don't see any red flags already—you are deluding yourself."

Efforts by the football community to clamp down on all the wagering are an exercise in hypocrisy.

The legal sports books also have seen hefty competition recently from offshore wagering websites. Authorities' attempts to crack down on those unsanctioned sites have been only sporadically successful.

Truthfully, efforts by the football community to clamp down on all the wagering are an exercise in hypocrisy. After all, the NFL has welcomed fantasy football into its world, going so far as to have official sites for such "gaming," while denying it is true betting.

In 2015, DraftKings was allowed to open its own lounges at three stadiums, homes of the Cowboys, Patriots, and Chiefs. FanDuel, meanwhile, signed sponsorship deals with 15 NFL teams.

"It's amazing," Eccles told *USA Today*. "It's surprised us how quickly everything has moved."

Again, *show me the money*!

The Helmet

Here, Wear This!

To think that in its original form, football was played helmetless.

And now, looking at today's football helmets, surpassed in sports only by the astronaut-like head coverings worn by race car drivers, safety would seem a given.

It's not, and there have been questions galore about helmets' protective nature, the necessary "give" in them, and whether, in some cases, they do more harm than good. Those doubts were most prevalent in the 1990s and early 2000s, when the practice of launching one-self into a blocker or ball carrier plagued football on the pro, college, and even high school levels.

That despicable maneuver pretty much has been eliminated from the field. Meanwhile, administrators on all of those levels have sunk millions upon millions of dollars, countless hours of scientific research and brainstorming into attempts to find the perfect helmet—something that doesn't exist and never will.

NO. 7

The first recorded use of the protective headgear came in 1893, when Joseph "Bull" Reeves of Navy was told by a doctor that he was risking "instant insanity" by playing the game without wearing anything to prevent head injuries. A cobbler designed a leather cap for Reeves.

Three years later, George Barclay of Lafayette College went to a harness maker for head-gear that included flaps. Still, such players were rarities and there were no rules governing helmets.

It wasn't until 1917 that a truly protective helmet was constructed, by Illinois coach Bob Zuppke, who understood the need for absorbing the impact from hits and collisions. His version included layers separated by cloth.

By 1920, professionals were wearing a soft leather version with ear flaps. A harder leather version came into use in the 1930s. (Think about what the Marx Brothers wore in

A leather helmet believed to have been worn by Gerald Ford at Michigan, 1932-1934

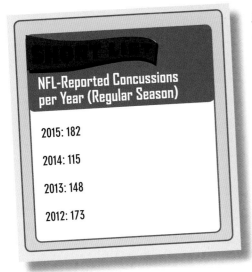

NFL-Reported Concussions per Year (Regular Season)

2015: 182

2014: 115

2013: 148

2012: 173

Horse Feathers.) They were relatively primitive, and not every NFL player was required to don them until 1943. Not until 1940 did they have chin straps, so keeping them snug to the head was difficult.

The NCAA, rather than the NFL, was ahead of the curve on requiring helmets, doing so in 1939 with a plastic device made by Riddell.

By the end of the 1940s, the "Leatherheads" were gone everywhere as the pros went to plastic helmets with internal padding. Although the face mask was invented in 1935, it took until 1955 to have the single face bar added. And by the early 1960s, some players—specifically defenders—had gone to the double face bar. Face masks became mandatory in 1962.

There remained much work to do, however: The plastic helmets didn't absorb enough energy and players' heads tended to rattle around inside—in part because of loose chin straps, still a problem today.

In 1971, air bladders were placed inside helmets, designed to soften impacts. Four years later, players began wearing full face masks.

The evolution continued in the 80s with the development of protective visors—Eric Dickerson was the first star to use one—and the first fully polycarbonate rendition in 1986. The polycarbonate was harder and more durable, and the true forerunner of the current helmets.

By the turn of the 21st century, the specter of concussions and head trauma that affected players over lengthy periods—some for the remainder of their lives—necessitated further research and improvements for the helmet. In 2002, Riddell came up with what it called the Revolution, which the company said was designed to reduce concussions and was more protective on hits from the side and back.

Nearly a decade later came the company's 360 helmet, again conceived to be more concussion-protective. Chin straps were upgraded to indicate the impact made on the head area and perhaps help identify injuries. One such strap uses an accelerometer to measure the force, duration, and direction of every hit on a player. The force of each hit is measured against a "head injury criterion" that can set off indicators such as a flashing LED when the severity of the blow suggests a better than 50 percent chance of a brain injury. Such technology is intriguing, though the regular use of such chin straps is uncertain.

Despite all of these advances, a variety of studies have shown that the safety qualities of helmets might not be keeping up with enhanced degrees of danger in the sport—particularly with players becoming bigger and faster, and hitting so much harder.

After a congressional committee wondered whether the NFL was making player safety issues a priority and criticized the league's research into equipment—particularly helmets—an independent survey was sanctioned by the league and the players' union in 2010. That study noted that modern helmets met all national safety standards, but that no helmet can prevent concussions. The findings urged more studies. "The study should be regarded as an initial step in learning more about the effectiveness of safety equipment," Commissioner Roger Goodell said in a memo to NFL teams obtained by The Associated Press. "It is not a definitive statement on helmet performance."

In 2014, the American Academy of Neurology released a study claiming that many current helmets were not properly made to protect players from concussions on hits from the

Helmets on average reduced the risk of traumatic brain injury by only 20 percent compared to not wearing a helmet.

side. The problem, the academy found, ranged across every level of football, and that helmets on average reduced the risk of traumatic brain injury by only 20 percent compared to not wearing a helmet.

"Alarmingly, those that offered the least protection are among the most popular on the field," said Dr. Frank Conidi, who co-authored the survey. "Biomechanics researchers have long understood that rotational forces, not linear forces, are responsible for serious brain damage including concussion, brain injury complications and brain bleeds. Yet generations of football and other sports participants have been under the assumption that their brains are protected by their investment in headwear protection."

So while the development and improvement of helmets for more than 120 years has been a game changer, such studies indicate more must be done.

The Greatest Game Ever Played

Baltimore Colts vs. New York Giants, NFL Championship Game, 1958

Can you believe there was a time when the NFL was not at the top of the list in sports popularity? A single game changed all that.

The NFL's championship game in 1958 between the Baltimore Colts and the New York Giants has been called "The Greatest Game Ever Played." It was every bit as dramatic as any in pro football history and had the fans screaming throughout. First the Giants took the lead. Then the Colts. Then the Giants. And then a tie for the first time in a title game. For the very first time, sudden death. All this before a national TV audience, another first.

"You couldn't come up with a scenario to beat the '58 game, even if you stayed up all night to plot it," said Raymond Berry, the Colts' star receiver. The 60,185 fans who packed Yankee Stadium on that December day would never forget it.

The Colts were the all-American success story behind quarterback Johnny Unitas, who came out of nowhere to become one of the league's biggest stars. Unitas was born in 1933 in the wake of the Depression that left many American families in dire straits. His father, who had a small coal delivery business, died when Unitas was four. His mother needed to support her four children. She went to school to learn how to be a bookkeeper.

The odds were against Unitas for any kind of success until he found his true calling as a football player. Unitas played his college ball at Louisville. He was drafted by the Pittsburgh

Baltimore Colts quarterback Johnny Unitas (19) in action.
Unitas led the Colts NFL championships in 1958 and 1959.

On a Quarterback's Relationship with his Coach

"You don't become a real quarterback until you can tell the coach to go to hell." —*Johnny Unitas*

AUDIBLE

Steelers in the ninth round in 1955, but didn't last long with the NFL club. The Steelers' coach, Walt Kiesling, told owner Art Rooney that Unitas couldn't remember the plays. The Steelers gave Unitas $10 and told him to buy a bus ticket home.

He was playing semipro ball in the sandlots for $6 a game when the Baltimore Colts offered Unitas a tryout. He joined the team in 1956, and with coach Weeb Ewbank, began one of the NFL's most special coach/player relationships.

Not that the two didn't have occasional disagreements. One of Unitas's most famous quotes regarding their relationship—about telling "the coach to go to hell"—was clarified in *Sports Illustrated*, which also quoted Unitas as saying, "I loved playing for Weeb [Ewbank], but sometimes I'd just ignore what he told me," Unitas told *Sports Illustrated*. "Early in my career he'd try to limit where I could throw against certain people."

Unitas's Colts debut was inauspicious, as he went 0-for-2 with an interception against Detroit. Two weeks later, starting quarterback George Shaw broke his leg. Enter Unitas.

Unitas finished the year with nine TD passes, including one that started a record 47-game touchdown streak. His completion mark of 55.6 percent was a rookie record.

The 1958 championship featured football legends.

Among the Colts: Unitas, Alan Ameche, Lenny Moore, L. G. Dupre, Raymond Berry, Artie Donovan, Big Daddy Lipscomb, and Jim Mutscheller.

For the Giants: Frank Gifford, Charlie Conerly, Kyle Rote, Alex Webster, Andy Robustelli, Mel Triplett, Sam Huff, Pat Summerall, and Roosevelt Brown.

The Colts wrapped up the Western Conference race early with a 9-1 record. The Giants had a more difficult time getting to the NFL championship game. They had to beat the Cleveland Browns twice, including a playoff game after the teams tied for first place in the

Eastern Conference with 9-3 records. Next stop, the NFL championship game. And one for the ages.

The Giants took a 3-0 lead in the first quarter on a 36-yard field goal by Summerall.

In the second quarter, the Colts demonstrated a clear superiority. On a 2-yard touchdown run by Ameche and a 15-yard TD pass from Unitas to Berry, the Colts took a 14-3 lead.

In the third quarter, the Colts were at the Giants 1 yard line with the chance to increase their lead. It was fourth down and in the huddle Unitas called for Ameche to take a handoff and throw a pass. Ameche mistakenly thought he was supposed to run the ball. He was tackled short of the goal line and the Giants went on offense.

The roar of the Yankee Stadium crowd got louder and louder as the Giants moved the length of the field to cut the Colts' lead to 14-10. In the fourth quarter Conerly connected with Gifford on a touchdown pass. Giants 17-14. Next came the most controversial play of the game.

Late in the fourth quarter, the Giants were trying to run out the clock for another championship. There were less than three minutes left.

Gifford, who had three fumbles in a frustrating afternoon, sought to redeem himself by picking up a first down on a sweep around the right side. And he thought he had gained enough yardage before he was tackled by Marchetti.

At the bottom of the heap of players, Marchetti screamed in pain. He had broken his leg. The Giants to this day claim the official was so distracted by Marchetti's screams that he had missed the actual placement of the ball and put it a few feet back of Gifford's forward progress.

"It was the worst placement I've ever seen," remembered Giants announcer Chris Schenkel.

Gifford yelled in protest, to no avail.

Unitas was back to work his magic with 1:56 left, and no timeouts.

Unitas completed a fourth-and-10 pass to Moore. Then he hit Berry for 25, 15, and 22.

With seven seconds left, Steve Myhra kicked a field goal to tie the game, 17-17.

All around America, people were huddled around their radios and television sets. Never had there been a tie in the championship game. Now, sudden death. The tension was electrifying.

The Giants won the coin toss but wound up punting. Unitas took the revived Colts 80 yards in 13 plays, including two third-and-long passes to Berry. With the game 8:15 into overtime, Ameche scored from the 1 to give the Colts their first championship.

Baltimore 23, New York 17.

Since the 19th century, college football had ruled the American gridiron scene. After the 1958 game, it became no contest. The NFL never looked back.

At the bottom of the heap of players, Marchetti screamed in pain. He had broken his leg.

The NFL Draft

"On the Clock" Becomes the Most Exciting Offseason Phrase for Fans

The NFL draft has become its own cottage industry, the third most popular pro football event, behind only Super Bowl Sunday and the opening weekend of the regular season.

Under Commissioner Roger Goodell, the draft has expanded to a three-day extravaganza, and beginning in 2015, it became a traveling circus, leaving its longtime home in New York City for Chicago where the proceedings that May rivaled Mardi Gras.

NO. **9**

Mock drafts have become so popular that Pat Kirwan of SiriusXM NFL Radio and CBS TV, a former NFL general manager and one of the most respected talent evaluators in the sport, has been asked to compile them the day after the Super Bowl. Yes, three months in advance.

Those bear hugs endured with a smile on his face by Goodell when first-rounders have their names announced? Goodell considers it "a privilege."

The draft has gotten so big that *two* networks, ESPN and NFL Network, televise every pick. All 256 of them.

"The interest on TV blows me away," says Mike Mayock, the NFL Network's draft guru. "Look at the ratings on both ESPN and NFL Network . . . and compare them to the NBA or NHL playoff games. The draft blows them away. *Playoff games.* I can't even begin to imagine that an event like the draft can overshadow a professional playoff game."

At the beginning of what has become a big-money phenomenon, the draft was, well, an offbeat idea in the brain of Bert Bell. Then the owner of the Philadelphia Eagles and later a league commissioner, Bell had tired of bidding wars between NFL teams for college talent in the 1930s. Searching for "a better way," he came up with a proposal that would change the face of pro and college football forever.

On February 8 and 9, 1936, the first draft was conducted in Philadelphia. As the *New York Times* reported: "Franchise owners crowded into Bert Bell's hotel room, shucked their

The set of the NFL 2010 Draft

jackets, and cleared the beds and bureaus for seating room. Bottles circulated, solemn oaths of league solidarity were taken, and the college stars were distributed." From that low-key scene grew the annual NFL Selection Meeting.

But the early growth was not substantial. The first pick was Jay Berwanger, the University of Chicago star halfback and the first Heisman Trophy recipient. The Eagles, figuring the top college player surely would be a star in the pro ranks, felt they had their franchise player in a sport dominated by the running game at the time. Berwanger had other ideas.

"I really wasn't interested in pro ball," he said. "They weren't paying any money, something like $100 a game. You couldn't blame them. This was following the Depression and nobody had any money."

So Philly traded the rights to Berwanger to Chicago, and team owner George Halas, one of the league's founders, set about persuading Berwanger to become a Bear. Berwanger asked for $25,000 for two years with a no-cut clause. Halas walked away.

Other top picks have balked through the years, even after the NFL became America's most successful sport. In 1979, Ohio State linebacker Tom Cousineau chose the Canadian Football League rather than join the Buffalo Bills. In 1986, Auburn's dynamic running back, Bo Jackson, opted for baseball rather than play for Tampa Bay. In 2004, Eli Manning didn't want to go to San Diego, which chose him first overall, and forced a trade to the New York Giants.

The draft has become the be-all and end-all for collegians. Indeed, finishing educations has become secondary as underclassmen populate the selections year after year. For decades, the NFL barred any non-senior from entering the draft. In 1990, under heavy pressure from player agents and the threat of lawsuits, the league relaxed its restrictions, letting juniors enter as long as they renounced their college eligibility. The first overall selection that year, Illinois quarterback Jeff George by Indianapolis, had a year of eligibility left.

Sitting in the green room, their agony was broadcast to millions.

Intrigue and espionage infiltrated proceedings in the 1960s when the AFL was established and began outbidding—or out-pirating—the NFL for players. It was common for pro team scouts, general managers, even owners to show up at the final contest of a collegian's career, often at a bowl game, seeking to sign a star who they had previously drafted. Some AFL and NFL teams wound up with the rights to specific players they had a better shot at signing than did their league partners.

How crazy did it get?

A Memphis tackle, Harry Schuh, was the prize sought by the Rams of the NFL and Raiders of the AFL in 1965. Raiders owner Al Davis told *USA Today* how he landed Schuh, who went on to a solid career in Oakland.

Schuh was sequestered in a Las Vegas hotel by Rams employee Harp Pool. "We had to pull an escapade," Davis said. "We had to get him out of the hotel."

The Raiders got word to Schuh they would take him wherever he wanted to go if he would bolt from the Rams' lair. His choice was Hawaii.

So, Davis explained, he walked through the front of the hotel to get the keys for Schuh's room. Pool was keeping a close eye on Davis, who was a decoy. Raiders assistants sneaked Schuh out of the back of the hotel and on to Hawaii for a week.

Such shenanigans are no longer required. But there's still plenty of drama, if not over the first pick, who often has agreed to a contract before his name is called out, then over how high-profile players slip down.

Three outstanding college quarterbacks were victimized by the draft free-fall: Aaron Rodgers, Brady Quinn, and Johnny Manziel. Their consternation was chronicled by the very TV networks that so popularize the draft: sitting in the green room, their agony was broadcast to millions.

Bert Bell might have been dismayed by the lack of compassion. But he would have been thrilled by the game changer the NFL draft had become.

SHORT LIST

The First Seven No. 1 Draft Picks in NFL History

Year	Player	Position	School	Team	Yrs Played	Pro Bowl
1942	Bill Dudley	HB	Virginia	Pittsburgh Steelers	9	3
1941	Tom Harmon	HB	Michigan	Chicago Bears	2	0
1940	George Cafego	HB	Tennessee	Chicago Cardinals	4	0
1939	Ki Aldrich	C	Texas Christian	Chicago Cardinals	7	2
1938	Corbett Davis	FB	Indiana	Cleveland Rams	DNP	-
1937	Sam Francis	FB	Nebraska	Philadelphia Eagles	4	0
1936	Jay Berwanger	HB	Chicago	Philadelphia Eagles	DNP	-

Concussions

The Football Plague of the New Millennium

NO. 10

Chris Borland was a promising linebacker coming off a strong rookie season with the 49ers. He seemed ready for stardom.

Instead, in 2015, after just one season in the NFL, he retired, fearing he might fall victim to the biggest medical problem in football: head trauma.

Concussion had become more than a buzzword in the sport. It had become a plague.

At 25, Borland was done.

And in late 2015, the film *Concussion*, starring Will Smith as Dr. Bennet Omalu, brought the issue of head trauma and its long-lasting effects to movie screens around the world.

No one disputes that football is a violent, collision sport. Safety measures have helped make the game less dangerous, but hardly safe. Nor will it ever be free of risk of long-term injury and illness.

Former Harvard football player turned professional wrestler Chris Nowinski lied about sustaining a concussion in the ring, and it led to the end of his athletic career. As he has noted in his current role as founder of the Sports Legacy Institute: "You know, when I got injured, and I continued to lie about my symptoms, it was out of ignorance. And it's very hard to be ignorant today. Everybody has heard about concussions. Everyone knows . . . at least some of us out there who think this is a major issue [in football]. People now have a chance to change what they expose their children to, to change their own course, to not lose their health out of ignorance."

Ignorance was ill-advised bliss for players for decades. Head injuries that caused players to become dizzy, disoriented, or to pass out were treated with smelling salts and other prehistoric methods, because no one fully recognized or understood the threat to overall health such trauma caused.

The Chicago Bears' Joe Zeller, helmetless, practicing with Red Grange (top), helmetless, in 1935

On Early Retirement

"I just honestly want to do what's best for my health. From what I've researched and what I've experienced, I don't think it's worth the risk." —*former 49ers linebacker Chris Borland, after retiring after his rookie year*

AUDIBLE

Indeed, thousands of football's veterans and their families filed lawsuits, collectively or individually, against the NFL or the NCAA and college administrators, saying they were misled or not informed of the dangers of head injuries. They accused those organizations of knowingly misguiding them.

After years of haggling as former players joined the legal proceedings, the NFL reached a settlement in 2013 agreeing to pay more than 5,000 plaintiffs and their families a total of $675 million. That seemed like a bargain for the league, and complaints that such a sum was woefully short of being fair eventually led to an increase in the settlement to about $1 billion.

Still, there were substantial disagreements, particularly from ex-players suffering from Alzheimer's, ALS, dementia, and other life-sapping diseases that many attributed to the hits they took on the field. Some have filed their own lawsuits against the NFL.

Most notable, perhaps, was the battle fought by the survivors of Hall of Fame linebacker Junior Seau, who took his own life in 2012. It was discovered that Seau suffered from CTE (chronic traumatic encephalopathy), a disease only discernible after someone has died and the brain is examined.

CTE is a progressive disease associated with repeated head trauma. More than three dozen NFL players have been diagnosed with it after their deaths.

"I think it's important for everyone to know that Junior did indeed suffer from CTE," Gina Seau, his ex-wife, told ESPN.com. "It's important that we take steps to help these players. We certainly don't want to see anything like this happen again to any of our athletes."

Yet concussions and head injuries are unavoidable in such a contact sport. The onus has fallen—as it should—to administrators, trainers, and doctors on all levels of the game, from youth football through high schools, colleges, and, of course, up to the NFL—as the Will Smith film *Concussion* so powerfully demonstrates.

USA Football, the national governing body for the sport, has instituted Heads Up Football, a program emphasizing removing the head from tackling. Backed by grants from the NFL, Heads Up Football has become an important and widespread safety initiative at the younger levels.

Rules changes throughout the sport have emphasized avoiding hits to the head to protect players. Launching—where a player leaves his feet and goes headfirst into an opponent with the crown of his helmet—was outlawed after it became the scourge of football. High hits to players in vulnerable positions have been banned. Game officials are instructed to flag any sort of contact with the helmet, even when it is inadvertent.

Just as significantly, concussion protocols have been established that nearly—but not entirely—guarantee that any player suspected of being concussed is removed from a game, examined on the sideline and then in the locker room/training room. He must pass those tests before being allowed to return to action.

In Super Bowl XLIX, even those precautions fell short. With New England rallying late and using a no-huddle, quick-tempo offense, Patriots receiver Julian Edelman caught a pass and was plastered by massive Seahawks safety Kam Chancellor. Woozy, Edelman remained on the field for the next snap; true concussion protocol wasn't followed.

Should a medical observer in the press box suspect a player has been concussed, he can order the game stopped.

That led to the NFL adding a medical timeout to its rules a few weeks later. Should a medical observer in the press box suspect a player has been concussed, he can order the game stopped and the player removed to undergo concussion testing.

"It came a little bit from the health and safety committee just saying, 'We've got these spotters [certified athletic trainers],'" NFL competition committee co-chairman Rich McKay explained. "'They've got a really good vantage point. They've got technology in their booth. They're communicating pretty well with our trainers and doctors, and we've got a pretty good rhythm going there.'

"Why would we miss a play when a player should come out?"

If it seems the NFL is all-in on reducing the risk of head trauma, well, it certainly is. If it appears late—and former players and their families agree—that, too, might be true.

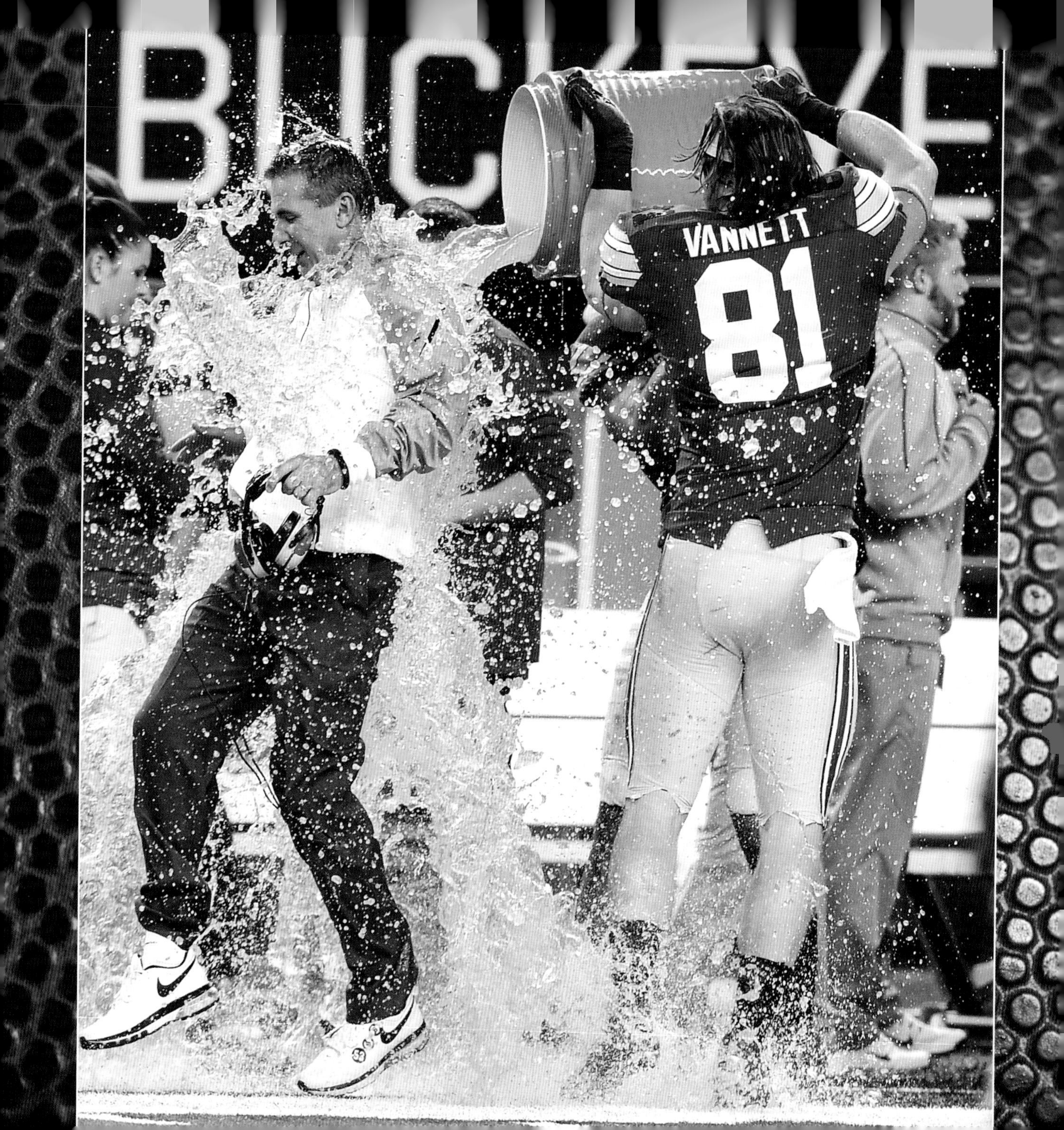
BUCKEYE
VANNETT
81

The BCS and College Playoffs

NCAA Division I Crowns a "True" Champion

Some said the BCS (Bowl Championship Series) was more BS than anything. The critics claimed the system launched in 1999 rarely worked.

Undisputed champions? In some years, perhaps, but certainly not in others.

Schools getting jobbed? Yearly.

Too much influence for the media, coaches, and other polls? Sure.

Ditto for the computers employed to calculate a formula that even rocket scientists couldn't fathom.

And even when the college football bosses at last seemed to get it right in the 2014 season with a four-team playoff, well, you'll never convince Baylor or TCU—or the entire Big 12—that the decision making was on-target.

Still, the days of teams winning the National Championship through a vote are gone, even if the days of voting to get into the playoffs remain. It was a long haul to get there.

Why? Try these two quotes from Bill Hancock, the man who defended like a 21st century Clarence Darrow the existence of the BCS and no playoff system. And the same man who now is executive director of, ahem, the College Football Playoff.

"College football has the best regular season of any sport, and the lack of a playoff is one big reason why. Millions of football fans this year tuned in to watch the season-opening game between Boise State and Virginia Tech because there was so much on the line—starting early in September," Hancock told *USA Today* in 2010.

And a few years later, when the playoff was established, he tweeted: "We think the four-team playoff doesn't go too far, it just goes the right distance. The event is very simple—the top 4 teams will play in a semifinal. . . . Let's settle it on the field once and for all."

A Gatorade bath for Ohio State Buckeyes head coach Urban Meyer during the fourth quarter in the 2015 National Championship Game

Well, yeah.

Going to a playoff system is a game changer in college football on many levels. It makes earning a conference championship a must. It pretty much makes a conference title game a must—for Baylor and TCU in 2014, the first year of the playoff, the lack of a Big 12 championship game helped keep both of them out of the four-team carnival that involved Florida State, Alabama, Oregon, and eventual winner Ohio State.

Both the Bears and Horned Frogs were damaged by very weak non-conference schedules that season. It all means that getting into the playoff will require big-time schools to play other big-time schools instead of the Prairie Views and Chattanoogas of the world.

Television, of course, can't get enough of the playoff. Not only was Ohio State's victory over Oregon the highest-rated program in cable TV history as ESPN drew more than 33 million viewers, but the programs it surpassed were the semifinals played on New Year's Day 2015 in the Sugar Bowl (Ohio State over Alabama) and the Rose Bowl (Oregon over Florida State), which held the records for 12 days.

Such overwhelming numbers are sure to lead to a clamor for more teams in the playoffs, and more highly watched games (read: more money for everyone involved).

And to think it took so long to get there.

Again, why? Penn State coach Joe Paterno campaigned for playoffs three decades before they came to pass. The reasons it took until 2014 are complex, centering on the profitability and tradition of the bowl games; supposed concern for the "student-athletes" having their football season extended; the power of the pollsters; broadcast partners protective of what their rights fees entailed; and the reluctance by some teams and conferences to give up longstanding alliances.

It wasn't until the 1998 season, one year after the creation of the Bowl Championship Series, that college football got it right. Sort of.

But by the close of the 20th century, it had become clear that letting national champions remain mythical, determined by media or coaches polls, was not what the public wanted. Sure, the controversies over who deserved to be No. 1 were juicy, but they were bad for the sport, focusing on the negative characteristics of the process. Such as there being split champions eight times; as recently as 2003, the major polls from The Associated Press (Southern California) and *USA Today* (LSU) had different winners. Such as not having a playoff.

In 1992, the Bowl Coalition was established, followed by the Bowl Alliance in 1995. Neither was all that effective in whittling down the contenders. It wasn't until the 1998 season, one year after the creation of the Bowl Championship Series, that college football got it right. Sort of.

A major stumbling block had been the strong tie-ins many conferences had with the bowl games, particularly the Big Ten and Pac-12 with the Rose Bowl. By incorporating four major bowls—Rose, Sugar, Orange, and Fiesta—into the BCS on a rotating basis, with one hosting the championship game every four years, the sport had come closer to Nirvana.

Except that every other bowl game not staging the title matchup was rendered less significant. Attendance and TV ratings for some of those games were damaged.

Still, progress was being made, and after Tennessee beat Florida State 23–16 in the Fiesta Bowl on January 4, 1999, there was virtually no debate about who was No. 1.

Yet Volunteers coach Phillip Fulmer still favored a playoff. "To have 11-1 football teams that get left out of the alliance, that really upset me," Fulmer said. "That shouldn't be that way. The best teams should have a chance to play [for a title] because the expectations are always high."

SHORT LIST

Co-National Champions in NCAA Division I (Mostly AP and UPI Polls)

1954 Ohio State / UCLA

1957 Auburn / Ohio State

1965 Alabama / Michigan State

1970 Nebraska / Texas

1973 Alabama / Notre Dame

1974 Oklahoma / Southern Cal

1978 Alabama / Southern Cal

1990 Colorado / Georgia Tech

1991 Miami/Washington

1997 Michigan/Nebraska

2003 LSU / Southern Cal

Undefeated teams such as Auburn in 2004 or one-loss squads too numerous to count never got a shot at the BCS Championship Game in subsequent seasons either.

By 2007, the plus-one game, played after the traditional bowls, was used to determine the national champion. Again, the same flaws generally hurt the system's credence. It was obvious what was needed: a playoff. In 2014, it happened.

"Although it was heavily criticized and misunderstood," said Hancock, "the BCS did everything it was intended to do and then some."

Perhaps. Or perhaps a playoff would have occurred had the BCS never been invented. Regardless, it changed the game in the 2014 season with a four-team format. Who knows how it will evolve?

Walter Camp

The Man Who Americanized an English Rugby-style Game

On a summer morning in New Haven, Connecticut, a runner made his way along the New Haven Green on a jaunt to Lighthouse Point. It was a ritual Walter Camp continued every morning. Sometimes Camp, determined to become physically fit, would extend his run even farther. He was determined to be in top shape so he could join the fledgling football team at Yale. It was 1876 and the Bulldogs were only in their fourth year, still trying to make their way through the murky waters of a new world of college football.

College football, American style, that is.

NO. **12**

Until 1869, football in America resembled English rugby. That is to say, running with the ball and tackling, and then ending up in crashing pileups. Nothing was out of bounds in these fast-moving, free-for-all contests. Then Rutgers played Princeton in 1869, in what has been largely regarded as the first official college football game in America.

Seven years later, college football was still struggling to become a distinctly American sport with its own personality.

Welcome Walter Camp.

Even while playing football for Yale from 1877 to 1882 and serving as captain, Camp was contemplating making the game different, distinctly homegrown. Later as a member of the football rules committee, Camp helped to shape the modern game:

- Give teams sequences of possession instead of having them randomly move the ball back and forth across the field as they did in rugby.

- Provide a system that required a team to go 10 yards on four downs to retain possession.

Walter Camp, "The Father of American Football," in his Yale senior class picture

On Walter Camp's Dedication to the New Sport of Football

"Camp was resourceful, courageous, thinking continually in terms of football, swiftly solving new situations, and indomitable." —historian Parke H. Davis in the 1925 football guide

AUDIBLE

- Eliminate the rugby scrum and establish a line of scrimmage.
- Establish an 11-man squad to replace the 15-man rugby teams.
- Create a position called center to snap the ball back to the quarterback.
- Devise a new scoring system including six points for a touchdown, three for a field goal, and two for a safety.
- Place numbers on players' jerseys.

Such creative thinking earned Camp the title of "The Father of American Football." The nickname stuck.

Camp, a natural athlete, excelled at, well, just about *every* sport at Yale: pitcher and captain of the baseball team; halfback and captain on the football team; a leader in swimming, winning races up to five miles; and a leader in the new game of tennis. There was no doubt which sport was closest to his heart: football.

Camp had a keen desire to win, but only by fair means and within the rules. Many of his innovations were aimed at making the game of football less brutal, with no one having an unfair advantage.

Because the sport was so new, there were constant challenges and questions every time the football team played. Camp helped solve the riddles.

He was on the field for Yale's first game against Harvard and captained the team three of the five seasons he was in the lineup. In that period, the Bulldogs lost only one game.

In 1880, Camp entered Yale Medical School. But he liked sports more.

In 1882 he left medical school and went into business, eventually becoming chairman of the board at the New Haven Clock Company. Still, he continued to serve as Yale football coach.

In five seasons as coach, his teams won National Championships three times, winning 67 of 69 games. Camp would also coach at Stanford, but it was at Yale that he made his biggest impact.

Americanizing football gameplay was a legacy, for sure. But there was more, much more.

In 1906, Camp was called to the White House by President Theodore Roosevelt, along with other top coaches, to deal with safety issues after a large number of football players died on the gridiron. This led to the start of the passing game and opened a whole new world for college football. The NCAA, today's college governing body of sports in America, also came out of those early coaches meetings.

Camp helped to develop the first All-America team to recognize the best college football players in the nation in 1889. Camp was not totally involved until 1898 when players from the west were selected. His selections from 1898 to 1924 were recognized as the official All-America team until his death in 1925. After Camp's passing, famed sportswriter Grantland Rice continued the tradition of the All-America team until 1948. It was a consensus All-America team until 1966, when the Walter Camp Football Foundation took over.

Each time, Camp took a position of leadership.

In 1881 football was in danger. There was talk of banning the game and going back to rugby.

The cause: the scrimmage rules. Princeton was meeting Yale with both teams undefeated. Princeton had figured out that if a team wanted to, it could hold the ball so its opponents never had a chance to score. The rules allowed it.

The Yale football team and the spectators were becoming extremely angry. Having spent good money, the spectators wanted to see some action.

In the second half, Yale's players decided they would also hold on to the ball. Now Princeton was angry. Noted as the "block game," it became one of the most detested contests of all time.

Camp came to the rescue. His famous "yards to go" rule was adopted on October 12, 1882.

The final score: 0–0 tie.

College football needed a savior. Camp came to the rescue. His famous "yards to go" rule was adopted on October 12, 1882.

"If on three consecutive fairs and downs a team shall not have advanced the ball five yards, nor lost ten, they must give up the ball to opponents at the spot of the fourth down." With all the measuring involved, it was decided the field be marked off in five-yard segments. Someone remarked, "By gum! It looks like a gridiron!"

Gridiron it was. Football had become truly American, thanks greatly to Walter Camp.

Red Grange

Bringing Football Out of the Dark Ages in 1920

During a time when professional football players were looked down upon because they played for money—and they didn't play for much, $100 to $200 a game—college coaches considered professionals no more than a bunch of ignoble roughnecks.

So after Red Grange, a three-time All-America running back, had played his last college game in 1925 for Illinois, it was expected that his football career had ended.

C. C. (Cash and Carry) Pyle had other ideas.

"A guy came up to me after a game and said, 'Kid, how'd you like to make a hundred grand?'"

Pyle's proposition: play professional football.

Compared to the college game, which was far more popular than the five-year-old pro football league, paid football was struggling for acceptance. The colleges were drawing sellout crowds. America was having a love affair with the college game, pure and untainted, with brilliant players such as Grange and popular teams such as Notre Dame's Fighting Irish, led by the legendary Knute Rockne.

Grange's college coach, Bob Zuppke, and his father advised him against playing pro ball.

But Pyle was a slick operator. He was one of the first of the sports agents, dapper in his tailor-made suits, derby hat, and cane. He presented a deal to Grange that was hard to turn down. Grange would be working for Pyle, and Pyle would lease him out to the Chicago Bears. The Bears would feature Grange in a 19-game barnstorming tour. The two teams in each matchup would take a fixed cut of each game's proceeds. Pyle and Grange would split the rest.

When he was at Illinois, Grange had cemented his popularity with an incredible performance against undefeated and top-ranked Michigan in 1924. The breakout occurred at the dedication of Memorial Stadium in Champaign.

NO.

Red Grange, December 1925: The Galloping Ghost who was "out to get the money."

SHORTCUT

The Original National Football Teams, 1922

Akron Pros, Buffalo All-Americans, Canton Bulldogs, Chicago Tigers, Cleveland Indians, Columbus Panhandles, Dayton Triangles, Chicago Bears, Detroit Heralds, Hammond Pros, Muncie Flyers, Chicago Cardinals, Rochester Jeffersons, Rock Island Independents

The first time he touched the ball, Grange raced 95 yards for a touchdown. He next scored on a 67-yarder, then added touchdown runs of 56 and 45 yards—all in the first quarter and within a period of 12 minutes. Later in the game, Grange scored another TD and passed for yet another to lead Illinois to a 39–14 victory over the Wolverines.

Talk about doing it all, he also held the ball on the point-after-touchdown kick, and played brilliantly on defense in those days when players went both ways.

He could write his own ticket to the pros—which he did.

"When I signed with the Bears," Grange recalled years later, "I would have been more popular had I joined the Capone mob."

College teams played to 50,000 while professional teams were lucky to get 10,000. Most big cities didn't want a professional team.

It was only after Tim Mara agreed to finance a team in New York that the Giants found a place in the Big Apple. That was 1925, and the fans were largely indifferent. Mara estimated he had lost $30,000 in his first year and was determined not to lose any more. Grange would be his salvation.

Harold "Red" Grange got his nickname from his hair color. He lost his mother at a young age and was unsure about the direction of his life. His father, a lumber dealer, insisted that he complete high school. He decided to show up for football practice.

"The sight of a new uniform for just the asking was too much to resist," he said in later years.

Grange would eventually make the number 77 famous while playing for Illinois from 1923 to 1925. At Illinois, Grange was known by a variety of nicknames, "The Galloping Ghost" among the most popular thanks to famed sportswriter Grantland Rice.

He was also known as the "Wheaton Ice Man" for carrying ice blocks in his offseason to work himself through school. He was a solid 6-foot, 185 pounds with breakaway speed.

Grange scored 31 touchdowns and chalked up 3,736 yards rushing, 575 yards passing, and 253 yards receiving while earning All-America honors for the Illini.

Grange played his last college game on a Saturday, gaining 235 yards against Ohio State. No sooner than peeling off his Illinois uniform was Grange off and running in a Chicago Bears jersey.

He signed his lucrative deal with the Bears on Monday, practiced on Tuesday and Wednesday, then opened against the Chicago Cardinals in Wrigley Field on Thursday, Thanksgiving Day.

Some 70,000 fans practically broke down the fences at the Polo Grounds.

What happened next was unprecedented for pro football. A sellout crowd of 36,000 jammed the ballpark. When Bears owner George Halas counted the receipts for the day, he was overjoyed at the huge payday. It was reported that the emotional Halas cried.

Grange was more pragmatic. "I'm out to get the money," Grange said, "and I don't care who knows it."

Halas didn't have any problems recouping his investment. To do so, he put together a tight schedule, including a December 6 game against the Giants in the Polo Grounds. A huge crowd showed up that day. *The Daily News* called the game "one of the most distinct social and financial successes the city has ever experienced."

Successful beyond his wildest dreams, Mara walked away with $40,000. No question about keeping the Giants and pro football alive now. Mara hung on to establish the Giants as one of the strongest franchises in the league along with the Chicago Bears, Chicago Cardinals, and Green Bay Packers.

"We played eight games in 11 days," Grange recalled years later. Some 70,000 fans practically broke down the fences at the Polo Grounds, and some of those figures set records for years. When the tour ended, Grange had earned the unheard of sum of $100,000.

But that was just the beginning of the money explosion.

As one of sports' super agents, Pyle rolled out the endorsements for his client—and the money kept rolling in: a candy bar, a sporting goods line, endorsement of a car. Pyle also got Grange a big-bucks movie deal.

Grange was thrilled, buying himself a $500 raccoon coat and a $5,000 car.

Grange finished his pro career in 1934. As one of its first superstars, Red Grange gave pro football credibility and recognition—not to mention financial power. Grange started the National Football League in the direction of today's domination of professional sports, with players bathed in fabulous big-money contracts.

All by himself—with some help from an agent—Grange had opened the door to a land of riches.

The Talent Finder

Gil Brandt, the Cowboys, and the Computer Age

Guru. Godfather. Genius.

Those descriptions often have been used to describe Gil Brandt, former scouting director for the Dallas Cowboys and then the NFL's draft consultant.

Brandt's wisdom, gathered from more than a half-century in pro football, was sought by owners, general managers, players, coaches, agents, media members, even commissioners. They all knew that it was Brandt and Cowboys general manager Tex Schramm who brought the NFL into the computer age.

And they did it in the 1960s.

"The New York Giants are still using that system," former Giants general manager Ernie Accorsi told *USA Today*. "I inherited it from George Young. We're still using it. Gil should absolutely be considered for the Hall of Fame."

Brandt's and Schramm's forward thinking helped Dallas string together 20 straight winning records (1966–1985).

"The great thing about Tex was he understood the need to think outside the box," Brandt said. "The Cowboys were willing to spend whatever it took and do whatever made sense to find the best players."

That meant going outside of American shores to discover kickers for America's Team. It meant stashing players in hotel rooms, even paying for a prospect to go to Hawaii, during the battle between the NFL and AFL for talent.

It meant being willing to wait for players with military commitments—particularly Roger Staubach. And it meant finding talent in other sports, most notably basketball.

Cowboys former vice president of player personnel Gil Brandt

On Gil Brandt's Draft Day Rockin' Eve

"Gil Brandt is to the draft what Dick Clark used to be to New Year's Eve, an American institution." —*Duke coach David Cutcliffe*

AUDIBLE

It meant personally meeting players (and their families) before they reached their senior years in college and were eligible to be drafted, creating a bond that made more than one prospect want to wear the star on his helmet.

Brandt did all of that, and much more.

Duke coach David Cutcliffe told *USA Today*: "Gil was the guy who went to the smaller colleges, finding diamonds in the rough. He spoke about evaluating character and making that count. That's a lost art."

Reliance on technology has spread across athletics, with no sport more entrenched in that world than football. Brandt always added a personal touch—decades after scouting players, he remembered the names of their parents and siblings and high school coaches—but always recognized there was data he and his team couldn't gather without the computers.

Most teams were still using handwritten or typed reports from their scouts while Dallas was collating reams of information on computer printouts. It was as if the other franchises were driving a Volkswagen Beetle and Brandt was at the wheel of a Corvette.

While everyone knew how great a college player Staubach was at Navy, winning a Heisman Trophy, the Cowboys' computers told them that a basketball player at Utah State named Cornell Green could make it in the NFL. Green played 13 seasons in the Dallas secondary, making five Pro Bowls and winning a Super Bowl.

What else did Brandt learn from the computers?

Try this:

"We all knew Texas had the best prospects and so many schools in other states—Oklahoma, Nebraska, Arkansas—went after those players," Brandt said. "What we would find out is about other areas that had top guys, and which areas to stay away from."

Brandt found out that Chicago's public schools produced very few potential stars, but the Chicago suburbs and parochial schools had lots of prospects. He got the same info about other locales across the nation.

He discovered that the traditionally African-American universities were filled with future NFL stars, so the Cowboys beat most other teams to them.

"We hired Dick Mansberger, who went to all these black schools, and we got a bunch of guys from Morgan State, Elizabeth City Teachers College, Johnson C. Smith, those kind of schools," Brandt said. "And these were very good players; it was kind of an unmined gold mine."

And this:

"In 1962, the Cowboys started using a computer to evaluate football players," Brandt told the *New York Times*. "We weighted the most important characteristics for success at each position, and it helped a great deal. One of the most important attributes that leads to an offensive lineman's success are long arms and big hands. This is just an example, because there are things at each position that lead to success or predict failure."

Gil Brandt discovered that the traditionally African-American universities were filled with future NFL stars.

And this:

The Cowboys sought a common denominator among prospects, regardless of position. They would feed such information as a players' size, speed, agility, strength, and statistics, all quantitative data, into the computer programs. But they also understood that so much more goes into identifying a winner: competitiveness, character, psychological makeup.

Technology couldn't do all that work. A scout's instincts were essential, too.

Brandt, for example, was right on the money when he predicted in 1998 that Peyton Manning would be a much better professional quarterback than Ryan Leaf. The Colts and Chargers owned the top two selections, and the debate was heavy over which one should go first to Indianapolis.

But from all his years in the sport, and his ability to recognize what makes the total package for an athlete, Brandt looked beyond the numbers. He discovered that Leaf had a questionable work ethic by talking to Leaf's high school coaches in Montana, with whom Brandt had a strong relationship. He had an even stronger connection to Leaf's coaches at Washington State, who provided more info.

"Once a scout always a scout," Brandt told *USA Today*. "Evaluating players is such a fascinating thing."

NFL Expansion

Professional Football Goes West, and South, and Midwest

The NFL decided long ago to stake a claim in all corners of the continental United States. Perhaps in the near future, they will venture across the Atlantic Ocean to London.

Pro football always has been about growth, and that doesn't mean simply organic growth. Other leagues, most notably the All-America Football Conference (AAFC) and AFL, have come along, and with mergers and assimilations, the NFL grew bigger and more widespread across the continent.

The NFL was established in 1922, changing its name from the American Professional Football Association, and fielding 18 teams in such sprawling metropolises as Canton, Ohio; Rock Island, Illinois; and Evansville, Indiana.

Expansion began almost immediately—by the next year, there were 20 franchises, although a few didn't play a full schedule.

From then through World War II, the NFL expanded and contracted as teams appeared and disappeared. Ever heard of the Louisville Colonels? Didn't think so: They lasted four games in 1926.

Some semblance of order began in 1933 with the league being split into Eastern and Western divisions and such familiar names as the New York Giants, Green Bay Packers, and Chicago Bears and Cardinals on the field of play. Still, some clubs came and went, and during the war years of 1942–1944, there were even combined squads.

Once the war ended and pro football began making inroads in the American sporting fans' consciousness—it was still far behind baseball, boxing, and college football in popularity—stability became the buzzword for NFL owners. There were 10 franchises from 1945 to 1949.

NO. 15

Fans of the Green Bay Packers—the team from the smallest city in the league—have witnessed and withstood every wave of league expansion.

SHORT LIST

The 1949 NFL Teams

Eastern Division:

New York Bulldogs

New York Giants

Philadelphia Eagles

Pittsburgh Steelers

Washington Redskins

Western Division:

Chicago Bears

Chicago Cardinals

Detroit Lions

Green Bay Packers

Los Angeles Rams

But there also was expensive player competition from the AAFC, which lasted four seasons, dominated by Paul Brown and his Cleveland Browns, who won every championship, and had clubs in non-NFL locales such as San Francisco, Baltimore, and Buffalo.

NFL commissioner Bert Bell saw the value of expanding westward long before Walter O'Malley and the Dodgers left Brooklyn for Southern California. Dan Reeves had moved his Rams from Cleveland to Los Angeles in 1946, and Bell wanted an accompanying franchise on the West Coast.

So the AAFC disappeared in a merger Bell helped engineer as the NFL absorbed the Cleveland, San Francisco, and Baltimore teams.

Thus began the semi-modern era of the NFL, with a steady roster of 12 franchises through the 1950s. Indeed, team owners might have been satisfied to remain with the setup had not another competitor—the American Football League—launched in 1960.

AFL organizers, led by Texas oil magnate Lamar Hunt, announced their intention to play games in 1960. Hunt had tried to buy and move the Chicago Cardinals to Dallas, but couldn't pull it off. "The NFL told him unequivocally that there would be no franchise in Dallas," Norma Hunt, his widow, told the *Dallas Morning News*.

So Hunt joined seven others to form the AFL, with a team in Dallas, while, quietly, Chicago Bears owner George Halas, chairman of the NFL expansion committee, went to Hunt's oil competitor, Clint Murchison, and offered him an NFL franchise for Big D. Hunt termed such action "sabotage."

"It's obvious what they're [the NFL] trying to do," he told the *Dallas Morning News*. "I think some congressmen and senators from states where we will have teams are not going to stand for it."

Even before the AFL had kicked off, the battle was on.

Murchison paid $1 million as an expansion fee, and his Cowboys easily outlasted Hunt's Texans, who moved to Kansas City after the 1962 season. By then, the Minnesota Vikings had paid a similar $1 million to join the NFL, boosting its membership to 14 and spreading its game to previously untouched territory.

That was part of the grand plan, of course, developed by Commissioner Pete Rozelle to conquer America. Rozelle already was raising the NFL's television profile at a skyrocketing rate.

The expansion fees would also skyrocket.

Miami (AFL) and Atlanta (NFL) were next into the fray, with the Dolphins paying a $7.5 million entry fee and the Falcons $8.5 million. The logic on those cities was clear: Florida was a rapidly growing market, and Atlanta was becoming the most cosmopolitan of southern cities. College football was king in both areas, but there was an appetite for the pros, too.

When merger talks got serious, it became apparent the NFL soon would grow exponentially.

New Orleans, a natural rival for Atlanta, came aboard the NFL in 1967 for $8.5 million. Cincinnati joined the AFL the next year for $8 million, knowing full well it would soon be in the NFL.

In 1970, all 10 AFL teams became part of the merged leagues. And for six seasons, the NFL had 26 very lucrative franchises.

But there were other regions to explore. The Pacific Northwest and Florida's Gulf Coast came in with the additions of Seattle and Tampa for $16 million apiece in 1976.

And the NFL rested. For nearly 20 years.

By 1995, the players had won free agency rights, and their salaries began to enlarge. Knowing how valuable franchises had become, the owners voted to bring in two more members: Carolina and Jacksonville—for the astounding expansion fee of $140 million each. After the Browns dumped Cleveland for Baltimore, Commissioner Paul Tagliabue promised to bring a team back to the loyal fans in the Dawg Pound. In 1999, the new-wave Browns were born, at a fee of $530 million. After the Oilers abandoned Houston for Tennessee, the league returned a team in 2002 for $700 million.

Today, any expansion talk centers on London or possibly Canada or Mexico, more new territories. Sure, the San Antonios and Las Vegases would love to become part of the NFL's fabric. But Commissioner Roger Goodell and the owners have their eyes abroad.

"London has done not only everything that we expected, but more than we expected," Goodell said before Super Bowl XLIX in 2015. "They're responding to the game better than we ever dreamed, with more enthusiasm, more passion. You see it every year. . . . Every event that we have explodes with interest.

Today, any expansion talk centers on London or possibly Canada or Mexico.

"So, their passion is obvious. We want to continue to respond to that fan interest, and if we do, we don't know where it will go, but I think there is great potential in London for the NFL."

That would be the most far-reaching football expansion of all.

Instant Replay

From Filling Dead Time to Fulfilling Official Reviews

Lindsey Nelson could handle just about anything in the broadcast booth. A veteran of countless games behind the microphone, from baseball no-hitters to last-second touchdowns, Nelson was a wordsmith nonpareil.

Yet when CBS producer Tony Verna told Nelson and his color analyst, Terry Brennan, what he had planned for the 1963 Army-Navy game, Nelson was at a loss.

"You're going to do what?" Nelson exclaimed when Verna mentioned the words instant replay.

Then Nelson turned speechless, perhaps for the only time in his Hall of Fame career.

Verna had been toying with the idea of repeating plays ever since he worked the 1960 Rome Olympics. He targeted football, which in his opinion had far too much time between action. How to fill up that time? Easy, Verna thought.

"The idea came to me out of frustration," he said. "Before replays, football telecasts were filled with dead spots. You spent a lot of time watching receivers walk back to the huddle after incomplete passes. It really destroyed the momentum of the telecast.

"Replays gave you something to show during the pauses. It seemed to make the game go faster."

Generations of sports fans have grown accustomed to immediately watching a replay. In pro and college football, replay even has become a part of the officiating process.

Verna's invention wasn't at first heralded as a breakthrough in telecasting. When he proposed using replay to his boss at CBS, Bill McPhail, himself an innovator, Verna was warned not to overdo it. There were concerns about it being invasive, or that live action could be missed while showing the replay. Nelson feared viewers would be confused.

Verna was undeterred. He lugged nearly a ton of equipment from New York to

Cue the *Jeopardy* theme song.

Explaining the First Ever Replay to a Television Audience

"This is not live! Ladies and gentlemen, Army did not score again." —*CBS broadcaster Lindsey Nelson during the 1963 Army-Navy game*

AUDIBLE

Philadelphia for the Army-Navy match, at the time still one of the classics of the college football season.

What he couldn't bring or use was new videotape; the network told him to reuse a reel, and he wound up with an old tape of *I Love Lucy* he was required to return to CBS; the first video replay in sports history was not preserved.

What would that play be? Again, easy, Verna thought.

"Roger Staubach was the Heisman Trophy winner and Navy was a strong team," he said. "We focused on Roger."

Much of the focus for this Army-Navy encounter naturally was on the recent assassination of President John F. Kennedy. The game had been moved back a week, and it was hoped the action would serve as a healing tool for the nation.

Deep into the contest, it appeared Verna's "toy" would never be unveiled.

"For most of the game, it didn't work," he said of the technology. "Then, late in the game, I heard the beeps straightening out and I said, 'Stand by, Lindsey.' And I hear the picture straightening out and I say, 'Go, Lindsey.'"

Staubach, however, was not on the field. Instead, the chosen play featured Army quarterback Rollie Stichweh scoring on a 1-yard run. Seconds after Stichweh surged into the end zone, Verna rolled the replay.

Touchdown, again! Very quickly, replay became a major part of any sports broadcast, with networks handling football games adding cameras specifically to show plays over again.

Eventually, slow motion, then super-slow motion and stop action, would be added to the equation. It's inarguable that video replay significantly contributed to the explosion in football's popularity on TV.

"I think it's hard to imagine viewing sports without instant replay," Verna said. "After [Army-Navy], every sporting event had to use it or people would complain."

That doesn't mean video replay is without its ills. It can be overdone, just as McPhail feared, and infringe on live action, particularly with the no-huddle offenses prevalent these days. And it can't always solve the plague of inconsistent officiating.

Even though replay became a staple of NFL and college football telecasts nearly a half-century ago, it took decades before it was applied as an officiating tool. As posted on the NFL's operations website, "The history of instant replay in professional football is filled with stops and starts; missteps and controversy; and modifications and improvements that continue to this day."

In 1978, replay was tested in some preseason games. Results were inconclusive.

"We still think we need a minimum of 12 cameras to get all the angles on every play," assistant supervisor of officials Nick Skorich said. "Electronically, I don't know if we are advanced enough yet."

Seven years later, a more effective system was tested in the preseason. There even was consideration for using it in the playoffs, but owners opted to delay.

But in 1986, it was adopted, with most reviews initiated by a replay official in the press box—except when on-field officials requested a review. End of story, right? No way.

Replay had been approved for one year, and only 10 percent of calls were reversed. It was approved on a yearly basis through 1991. Then the owners dumped replay, citing in-game delays and not enough corrected calls.

By 1996, the clamor to get back to the modern age was so loud that another preseason test was authorized. This one included coaches' challenges for the first time.

In 1999, fresh with the image of a blown call in a Seahawks-Jets game that probably cost Seattle a play-off berth, team owners approved reinstating replay, again for one season. It worked effectively, and in 2007 it was approved permanently—although with yearly tweaks to upgrade replay's impact.

In 1999, fresh with the image of a blown call in a Seahawks-Jets game that probably cost Seattle a playoff berth, team owners approved reinstating replay.

Thirty-two years after Verna, who died in 2015, presented video replay, the Directors Guild of America honored him with its lifetime achievement award in sports directing.

"With the creation of instant replay 50 years ago," guild president Paris Barclay said, "Tony changed the future of televised sports, and sports direction, forever."

Bowl Games

Rose, Orange, Sugar, Sun, Cotton, and Beyond

Today we have Bowl mania.

First there was the Rose Bowl, the "Granddaddy of Them All." Then followed the Orange, the Sugar, the Sun, and the Cotton. They were so successful that many other bowls followed their lead.

The Rose Bowl game was first played in 1902 in Pasadena, California. And it was the last time it was played for 14 years. The humiliation of it all: Stanford, the local team, was embarrassed by visiting Michigan, 49–0. Goodbye football, welcome back chariot races.

On New Year's Day in 1890, members of the Valley Hunt Club had paraded their flower-bedecked horse-and-buggies through the streets of Pasadena. The parade continued through the years and became known as the Tournament of Roses. In 1901, the president of the Tournament of Roses wanted to publicize his little village's floral festival. What better idea than a college football game featuring the best of the East against the best of the West?

Michigan and Stanford battled (if you could call it that) before 8,000 fans. Stanford conceded defeat with eight minutes left in the game.

That was the end of the football experiment in Pasadena. At least for a while. As football became more popular in ensuing years, there was renewed interest in an East-West game to accompany the tournament. In 1916 the Rose Bowl was reborn with a match between Washington State and Brown University.

This time the host team was victorious, 14–0. Football in Southern California was home to stay. The game was notable not only for the rebirth of the Rose Bowl, but the appearance of Fritz Pollard. Pollard, who would be inducted into the College Football Hall of Fame and the Pro Football Hall of Fame, was the first African American to play in a Rose Bowl game.

NO. 17

The "Granddaddy of Them All"

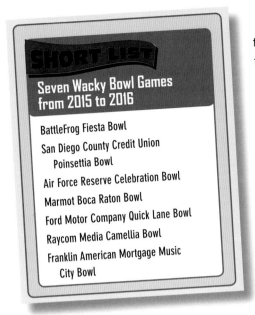

SHORT LIST

Seven Wacky Bowl Games from 2015 to 2016

BattleFrog Fiesta Bowl

San Diego County Credit Union Poinsettia Bowl

Air Force Reserve Celebration Bowl

Marmot Boca Raton Bowl

Ford Motor Company Quick Lane Bowl

Raycom Media Camellia Bowl

Franklin American Mortgage Music City Bowl

A fast-deteriorating Tournament Park had featured the football games until that time. A new stadium, patterned after the Yale Bowl, was built in Pasadena, a short drive from Los Angeles. It sat in a dry river bed called the Arroyo Seco, which had previously been a dumping ground, its west bank at the foot of the Linda Vista Hills. In the distance, the San Gabriel Mountains offered a beautiful view from the stadium. Harlan "Dusty" Hall, the tournament's press agent, was credited with coining the name "Rose Bowl" for the stadium.

The Rose Bowl game between Southern Cal and Penn State in 1923 marked the first time the contest was played in today's stadium. Traffic was a problem even then. The Penn State team, stuck in gridlock, arrived 45 minutes after kickoff was scheduled. The game continued late into the evening as the sky darkened. Southern Cal defeated the Nittany Lions 14–3 as sportswriters, it is said, lit matches to complete their stories.

One of the most memorable plays in Rose Bowl history occurred in 1929. Georgia Tech and California, two defensive giants, were locked in a classic, low-scoring game in the second quarter. Georgia Tech had the ball in the vicinity of its 30 yard line. Rambling Wreck running back John Thomason was hit hard by California's Benny Lom and dropped the ball.

Roy Riegels, California's star halfback and center, scooped up the ball and headed toward the Georgia Tech goal line. Avoiding tacklers, Riegels got turned around.

"I was running toward the sideline when I picked up the ball," Riegels later told The Associated Press. "I started to turn to my left toward Tech's goal. Somebody shoved me and I bounded right off into a tackler. In pivoting to get away from him, I completely lost my bearings."

"Stop! Stop!"

Riegels heard that from a teammate as he headed toward the California end zone, the wrong end zone. He finally realized something was wrong when he was tackled at the 1 yard line by one of his own teammates!

Riegels's blunder was turned into a safety for Georgia Tech, giving the Rambling Wreck a 2–0 lead at the half. Although Riegels played a ferocious second half, his mishap was the margin of victory for Georgia Tech, an 8–7 winner. And Riegels would forever be attached to one of the most infamous tags in football history: Wrong-Way Riegels.

In 1931, when Alabama faced Washington State, the Rose Bowl Stadium was enlarged from a "U" shape to a larger oval seating 81,000. The Rose Bowl would eventually fill its capacity to 92,542 as it became one of the best-known football stadiums in America with yearly sellout crowds.

Miami also was trying to attract winter visitors. The city was still struggling after a collapsing land boom and destructive hurricane in 1926.

So city fathers invited Notre Dame, with the popular Four Horsemen, to play an exhibition game.

Then, copying the Rose Bowl success, Miami businessmen staged a Festival of Palms Bowl in 1933, which was later renamed the Orange Bowl.

Before kickoff, an automobile appeared on the field, an outsized football on its roof. A cannon boomed, the football opened, and dozens of pigeons flew out, to the delight of the spectators.

A cannon boomed, the football opened, and dozens of pigeons flew out, to the delight of the spectators.

Miami, in the role of underdog, shocked visiting Manhattan College 7–0.

Other bowl games continued to sprout in warm-weather sites around the country. The Sugar Bowl in New Orleans debuted in 1935, the Sun Bowl started inviting teams to El Paso, Texas, in 1936, and the Cotton Bowl was launched in 1937 in Dallas.

With all the bowl games on the New Year's Day calendar in 1937, an Associated Press story was headlined in newspapers: Bowl Grid Games Are Here to Stay.

Indeed. The proliferation and commercialization of bowl games had only just begun, with sponsors attached to many bowls in the 1980s.

In the 1990s, the Rose, Orange, Sugar, and Fiesta came together as part of the Bowl Championship Series (BCS) to determine the national champion.

More changes were coming with a four-team playoff system at the end of the 2014 season. A staggering number of 41 bowl games were played by 82 different schools for the 2015 season, just about every game featured live on ESPN's various outlets. Go 6-6 during a season and watch how many bowl games want you!

With television and sponsor support, the Bowls just keep on coming.

Roger Goodell

A Commish Tackles NFL Rules Breakers and Scandals

When Roger Goodell took over as NFL commissioner from Paul Tagliabue in 2006, he made a vow. His primary objective: player safety.

Instead, Goodell wound up as the "Discipline Domo," cracking down on misbehavior that, at times, ran rampant through pro football.

NO.

Yes, it was a scant minority of the nearly 2,000 players in the league who were messing up. But to much of America—particularly in a social media age that blew up during Goodell's stewardship—it seemed as if every team had a bad guy.

So it became Goodell's chore, even his calling, to clean up a league for which he had worked since his college days. Cleaning it up on all levels—nailing players, coaches, and franchises.

In the wake of Steelers quarterback Ben Roethlisberger drawing a six-game ban (later reduced to four) for an alleged sexual assault that violated the NFL's personal conduct policy, Goodell addressed incoming players for 2010 at a rookie symposium. Sadly, it was emblematic of many speeches he would find necessary to give in the succeeding years.

"I talked on personal conduct. I didn't speak about anyone in particular in that case," Goodell said. "But I did talk about what I call protecting the shield. My job is to protect the integrity of the NFL and to make sure the game is as safe as possible."

He added that the personal conduct policy is "designed to protect those players and their reputations, because I think we have a bunch of great guys in the league."

And some not-so-great characters.

There were Spygate, Bountygate, and Deflategate—all tiresome word choices, but all befitting scandals that rocked the league.

Roger Goodell at 2009 NFL Draft

On Working in the National Football League

"I have stated it many times: Being part of the NFL is a privilege. It is not a right." —*NFL commissioner Roger Goodell*

AUDIBLE

There were, in a span of months, the cases of Ray Rice, Greg Hardy, and Adrian Peterson, the biggest headliners in 2014 and 2015 when a seeming epidemic of bad behavior struck the NFL.

In the middle of it all, always, was Goodell, attempting to protect that shield even as others tarnished it so badly. Less than a decade into his tenure, Goodell's biggest impact on the NFL came from how he would come down on rules breakers.

Waves of criticism accompanied every move, too, describing him as everything from "heavy-handed," to "judge, jury and executioner."

At one point, tackle Eric Winston, the president of the players' union, said: "Hey, even the worst bartender at spring break does pretty well. Think about it, a 2-year-old could [be commissioner] and still make money."

Winston later apologized, but the relationship between Goodell and the players already was irreparably damaged.

It wasn't so great with several franchises, either.

Here's why:

- In 2006, Goodell suspended Titans defensive tackle Albert Haynesworth for five games for stomping an opponent.

- The next year, Goodell fined Patriots coach Bill Belichick $500,000 for spying on the Jets' defensive signals. The New England franchise was also fined $250,000.

- In 2011, the league locked out the players in a dispute that lasted more than four months and endangered regular-season games. When a new contract was reached, Goodell kept his powers in overseeing all personal conduct issues. The union capitulated in negotiations on the topic, then rued doing so when it recognized how few its options were during disputes over punishment Goodell administered.

- The next year came the Saints' bounty scandal, one of the ugliest incidents in sports history. Goodell fined the team $500,000; stripped second-round draft picks in 2012 and 2013; suspended coach Sean Payton for the entire 2012 season for, basically, a lack of institutional control; barred assistant coach Gregg Williams indefinitely for running the bounty program that rewarded Saints defenders for "knockout hits" and tackles that injured opponents; suspended another assistant coach, Joe Vitt, for six games, and New Orleans general manager Mickey Loomis for eight games; and banned four players, including linebacker Jon Vilma for a full season. The coaches and Loomis served their full sentences, but the players eventually had their suspensions vacated by, of all people, Tagliabue, who had been appointed by Goodell as an arbitrator in the case.

- Indianapolis Colts owner Jim Irsay was docked $500,000 in 2014 for violating the personal conduct policy by possessing illegally obtained prescription medications.

And then there was Rice. And Peterson. And Hardy.

Goodell originally suspended Rice for only two games for hitting his fiancee in a casino elevator in Atlantic City. When video of the incident went viral, Goodell realized how lenient he'd been. Amid a public outcry that included calls from women's organizations for Goodell's resignation, he unilaterally imposed a new conduct policy calling for a six-game ban for an initial violation. He also banned the running back from the league, a suspension later overturned.

Amid a public outcry that included calls from women's organizations for Goodell's resignation, he unilaterally imposed a new conduct policy.

Vikings star running back Peterson pleaded guilty to hitting his 4-year-old son with a switch, and wound up spending 15 games on a commissioner's exempt list while paid his full salary. Goodell eventually suspended him until the following April, a court overturned it, and Peterson went back on the exempt list for the remainder of his "sentence."

Carolina pass rusher Hardy was found guilty on misdemeanor domestic violence charges that were dismissed after his accuser could not be located by prosecutors. He played in the 2014 season opener, then went on the exempt list, too.

Goodell suspended Hardy, who had moved to the Cowboys, for 10 games to start the next season, and the union promptly went to court to fight it.

Through it all, knowing full well more such cases would crop up, Goodell held firm on his role in changing the personal conduct environment.

"The policy is comprehensive," Goodell said. "It is strong. It is tough. And it is better for everyone associated with the NFL."

The NFL vs. AFL Bidding Wars

The 1960s' Battle for Top College Talent

This was war, pro football style.

No one had ever posed a serious threat to the NFL before. In three decades—the 1920s, 1930s, and 1940s—a league calling itself the AFL or AAFC tried to make a go of it against the NFL. All failed.

Now the NFL faced real competition from another start-up maverick league with tons of money that simply wouldn't go away.

A big reason for that was Lamar Hunt, a Texas oilman's son who had come out of college with his heart set on owning a football team. The 27-year-old Hunt's bid for an expansion franchise in Texas was rejected by the NFL. But you don't say no to a multimillionaire.

What did Hunt do? He just started another league.

He discovered that Bud Adams also wanted to buy the Chicago Cardinals and move them to Houston. That never happened, so Hunt gave Adams an opportunity to join the brand-new AFL. Adams eagerly accepted and joined an eight-team league that owners referred to, tongue-in cheek, as the "Foolish Club."

When Hunt and Adams announced at a news conference the formation of the American Football League, other eager "fools" rushed in to join them.

The talent hunt began. Adams landed the first blow to the NFL by signing Billy Cannon, the two-time All-America running back at LSU and winner of the Heisman Trophy.

Cannon had been drafted and signed by the Los Angeles Rams for $50,000, but a phone call to Cannon's trainer at LSU changed minds when Adams offered to pay twice as much. They worked out a three-year deal, with a plan to sign the contract after the Sugar Bowl on January 1, 1960.

Joe Namath rejected the NFL for a record $400,000 contract with the AFL's New York Jets.

SHORT LIST

The Original Eight AFL Teams (after some adjustments)

Dallas Texans * Denver Broncos * Houston Oilers * Los Angeles Chargers * Boston Patriots * Buffalo Bills * Oakland Raiders * New York Titans

Adams was ready to make Cannon pro football's first $100,000 player. But Cannon had another demand: a Cadillac for his dad. Adams took Cannon to his house for a home-cooked meal. Cannon was important to the AFL because he would legitimize the new league. So after the meal, Adams gave Cannon the keys to his wife's car. "She wasn't too happy about that," said Adams.

The war was on.

Cannon had signed with two teams, so the Rams went to court. The Oilers won because the Rams had signed Cannon before he had finished his college career. A newspaper headline read: Cannon Now Is Free to Play with Oilers in New Loop.

AFL 1, NFL 0.

There were other double signings and lots of trickery between the two leagues.

Both organizations used the practice of "babysitting" to protect players they wanted to sign. They would hide players, sometimes in hotels, so that the other league couldn't find them.

Barron Hilton, the owner of the Los Angeles Chargers, used his hotel chain to help all the AFL teams. "We could get these kids the biggest suite in the hotel and when their parents came in to visit, they were staying in the presidential suite," said AFL official Al LoCasale. "That created an aura that was helpful, and word got around among the players."

The AFL was a rebel league and attracted fans who were shut out of the sold-out NFL, or who just began to see a symbol for rebellion against the stodgy NFL and its boring style of ground-oriented play.

The AFL meant high-scoring, wide-open games featuring dramatic pass-oriented action. It was fun to cheer on the AFL's stars, many not deemed worthy of the NFL; others like Mike Garrett and Joe Namath were adored because they had rejected the NFL.

While both leagues recruited in the larger schools, which were mostly white, the AFL aggressively targeted small black schools.

"The NFL didn't have to go to those smaller schools. The AFL went after those players because they wanted to and they needed to," said Lionel Taylor of the AFL's Denver Broncos.

With Cannon and quarterback George Blanda, the Oilers won the first two AFL titles and played in two more championship games that first decade.

The new league set up mostly in cities that didn't have an NFL team. Even so, in its first year it lost money.

Hunt was not discouraged. "We felt we were going to be in the football business for a long period of time," said Hunt. And even though he lost $1 million, his dad, H. L. Hunt, said jokingly, "Well, at that rate, he can only go another 100 years."

Help for the AFL was just around the corner, from TV. In June of 1960 the league signed a five-year deal with ABC, which at that time was noted for its college football coverage. It guaranteed the AFL better financial footing, and ensured that every AFL market would have a televised game each Sunday.

The 1963 AFL championship game, in which San Diego beat Boston 51–10, created a tremendous amount of interest from the networks. That led to a $36 million contract over five years with NBC.

Now the upstart league was not going away. But there was bickering among NFL owners. Chicago Bears owner George Halas, one of the NFL founders, and Green Bay Packers coach Vince Lombardi were particularly opposed to a merger. Escalating salary wars and signing bonuses were hurting both leagues, though, and NFL commissioner Pete Rozelle ordered owners to work out something.

Dallas Cowboys general manager Tex Schramm was given the go-ahead to settle the issue with Hunt, whose team had moved from Dallas to Kansas City in 1963.

"They met in secret," remembered Gil Brandt, who was vice president of player personnel of the Cowboys from 1960 to 1989. "They met in rental cars, in parking lots so they could talk in absolute secrecy. They knew if word got out of a possible merger, there was too much that could go wrong."

As merger talks continued, Al Davis, then managing general partner of the Raiders, suggested the NFL move three teams to the AFL. The idea was rejected by the collective NFL—until Davis further suggested the teams receive $3 million each for making the move.

Help for the AFL was just around the corner, from TV. In June of 1960, the league signed a five-year deal with ABC.

"When the money went on the table, it was like barracudas going after raw meat," said Cincinnati owner Paul Brown at the time.

The Steelers, Browns, and Colts headed to the American Football Conference, which was renamed in 1970 when the merger was done. It was the beginning of a new era in professional football.

Al Davis

Rebel, Iron-Clad Iconoclast

There is no easy way to describe Al Davis. He has been called a Machiavellian figure by his enemies and a genius by his admirers.

It may not be entirely true to say that the Raiders franchise, in both Oakland and Los Angeles, began and ended with Davis. But it's close enough.

Following Davis's arrival in Oakland in 1963, the Raiders began their ascension in pro football. "Just win, Baby"—that was Davis's motto. And his Raiders did, a lot. From a 1-13 record the year before his arrival in Oakland, Davis's first Raiders team went 10-4. It wasn't long before the Raiders started winning championships, creating one of the NFL's first true dynasties in the 60s, 70s, and 80s.

NO. 20

Before he died at his home in Oakland in 2013 at the age of 82, Davis's teams had won 15 division championships, four conference titles, and three Super Bowls. He made five Super Bowl appearances overall with the Raiders in a variety of capacities, first as a coach and then GM and owner. Davis also found time to serve as commissioner of the upstart AFL for a year in 1966, playing a major role in the merger with the NFL.

He won both on and off the field.

"He was our first real success story," said George Ross, who was sports editor of the *Oakland Tribune* when Davis first came to town. Yes, just in basic economic and social terms he meant something important to a city with an inferiority complex.

An impatient man, Davis got things done in a hurry. It didn't take him long to challenge the popular San Francisco 49ers for the locals' loyalty. Suddenly, Raiders stickers could be seen sprouting all over San Francisco.

Davis grew up in Brooklyn, New York, a big sports fan with a passionate desire to go into sports management. He had a spotty college career, moving from college to college trying to find an athletic program he liked. "I didn't get along with coaches," said Davis, who

Oakland Raiders quarterback Ken Stabler (12) hands off to
Mark Van Eeghen (30) during Super Bowl XI.

On Sports Genius

"There is nobody who is smarter about football than Al Davis. Nobody. Period. Coaches. Owners. Players. Al Davis is the smartest man in all of sports." —*Raiders Hall of Famer Willie Brown*

AUDIBLE

played baseball and football. He graduated from Syracuse with an English degree. "I remember thinking, what am I studying English for when all I want to do is coach?" So coach he did.

His first job was at Adelphi on Long Island, then in the Army. Davis, a private, coached one of the most powerful football teams in the military, Fort Belvoir.

The experience was valuable. He joined the Baltimore Colts as an assistant, then went on to The Citadel, and finally Southern Cal before leaping to the pros with the San Diego Chargers.

Next stop: Oakland.

"I always wanted to take an organization and make it the best in sports," Davis said. Davis admired the Brooklyn Dodgers for breaking the color line in baseball with Jackie Robinson. And he would make his own mark in this regard in football when he hired Art Shell, a former Raiders lineman, as the first African American to coach in the NFL. Davis also hired Tom Flores as the NFL's first Latino coach, and Amy Trask as the NFL's first female chief executive.

"It is a historic event and I understand the significance of it," Shell told the *Los Angeles Times*. "But the main thing is, I know who I am and I'm proud of it . . . But I'm also a Raider and I don't believe the color of my skin entered into this decision. . . . If you know Al Davis and you know this organization, you'll understand that."

Davis's style could be described as imaginative and unconventional. Few figures had the impact on pro football that Davis did. He wore many hats—scout, assistant coach, head coach, general manager, owner, and commissioner. And did all the jobs remarkably well.

Players and associates point to Davis's knack for judging talent as the foundation of his success. Said Raiders Hall of Famer Gene Upshaw, who was president of the NFL Players

Association until his death in 2008: "When I came to the team I had never played offensive guard in my life. [He played tackle.] "Same thing with Todd Christensen. Al made him a tight end. Al would always do what it takes to win."

Davis also had a knack for recruiting. At one point during the AFL-NFL wars over talent, Davis signed several star collegians away from the NFL, including quarterbacks Roman Gabriel and John Brodie. Davis's success in signing those top players convinced NFL owners to come to the table in the 60s and talk about a merger.

He didn't care about an athlete's unsavory reputation or his difficult behavior, and there were plenty of those types of players through the years. He signed them, in some cases rehabilitated them, always giving them a chance to be successful. Some had allegations of criminal behavior, drug use, gambling, and other misbehavior.

If the roster rap sheet weren't enough, the Raiders' colors were chosen by Davis to intimidate: silver and black. Davis had always liked the black worn by the Army Black Knights football team, so he made that the primary color with the Raiders. The team insignia was dramatic: a shield emblazoned with the image of a pirate in a football helmet wearing an eye patch in front of crossed sabers. It reflected the take-no-prisoners style of play he emphasized, featuring brutal physical force on defense, speed, and long passing on offense.

The team insignia was dramatic: a shield emblazoned with the image of a pirate in a football helmet wearing an eye patch in front of crossed sabers.

"I don't want to be the most respected team in the league," Davis said in 1981. "I want to be the most feared." And so he was, by owners as well as teams. It was best not to get on the wrong side of Al Davis.

Among his most contentious confrontations was a contract dispute with Marcus Allen. Davis made sure Allen played less and kept the superstar running back mostly on the bench for two years. Allen then played the last five years of his 16-year NFL career with Kansas City. Allen, who would go on to earn a place in the Hall of Fame, wasn't the only notable feud opponent for Davis. After a lengthy legal battle with the NFL, Davis moved the team to Los Angeles in 1982, then back to Oakland in 1995.

Loved or hated, Davis had the right formula for success.

"He's a true legend of the game, whose impact and legacy will forever be a part of the NFL," said NFL commissioner Roger Goodell.

NFL Films

A Groundbreaking Approach to Presenting the World of Pro Football

Ed Sabol came upon The Voice of God in a Philadelphia tavern.

Sabol and his son Steve also came up with NFL Films. The elder Sabol, who died in 2015, is in the Pro Football Hall of Fame for his vision and creativity, and his son, who passed away in 2012, soon might follow.

Yet the spoken words of John Facenda always have defined the innovative media company. "We had some bad teams when I was here," former Philadelphia Eagles general manager Jim Murray told the *Philadelphia Inquirer*. "But NFL Films could take two of our highlights, get John Facenda to announce them, and make us look like Super Bowl contenders."

No one is sure who honored Facenda with his sobriquet, but it's a fit.

Facenda, a former TV anchorman in Philly, was at the bar watching one of Ed Sabol's productions in 1965 when "I started to rhapsodize about how beautiful it was. . . . [Ed] came up to me and asked, 'If I give you a script, could you repeat what you just did?' I said I would try."

Try? Facenda's rich voice, tinged with drama, came to individualize NFL Films.

Of course, brilliant scripts and powerful music accompanied the mesmerizing film (and later video). For decades—even now—whenever the opening of Steve Sabol's poem "The Autumn Wind" hits the airwaves, there's no question who The Voice of God is worshipping:

> The Autumn wind is a pirate
> Blustering in from sea
> With a rollicking song he sweeps along
> Swaggering boisterously.
> THE RAIDERS!

Camera crew for the NFL Films series *Hard Knocks*

By the time Facenda died in 1984, NFL Films' masterful artistry was so established that the Sabols were branching out beyond football, eventually filming major sporting events such as the World Series, NBA Finals, Stanley Cup Finals, Kentucky Derby, and Wimbledon.

They also would take on non-sports projects with the same imagination and invention that they devoted to the gridiron, producing everything from rock concert videos to educational films, even aiding police departments to analyze surveillance video. Indeed, NFL Films' first major non-football assignment was for NASA in the 1970s.

Naturally, though, the Sabols' greatest work involved what else but the NFL. As it boasts on its website, NFL Films was the first to:

- hire a woman executive in the NFL (Inez Aimee);

- wire coaches and players for sound;

- use ground-level slow motion;

- use 600-millimeter lenses in sports cinematography;

- edit sports films to pop music;

- use reverse angles replays;

- produce "Follies" films;

- score original music for sports films;

- use graphics to analyze game tactics and strategy;

- use montage editing in sports.

More than 100 Emmys later, NFL Films is universally recognized as *the* production company for sports.

And to think it all started when Ed Sabol, who described himself then as an "amateur moviemaker," spent the princely sum of $3,000 in 1962 for the rights to film the NFL Championship at Yankee Stadium between the Packers and Giants.

The Sabols understood long before reality television stormed the tube that sports were the true reality TV.

Then the elder Sabol needed to put together a staff. He brought Steve home from Colorado College, they formed Blair Motion Pictures, named after Ed's daughter, and hired a film crew.

Come Sunday, December 30, temperatures plummeted. Cameras broke, lenses freezing. Film cracked. Sabol sensed a failure.

"At that particular moment, I was not interested in doing another game nor concerned about the future," he told CNN. "I just wanted to get out of the stadium, get home and warm up."

But his fears were totally unwarranted. The Sabols' use of color film from a variety of cameras and angles, along with slow motion, dramatized the action. Close-ups of Vince Lombardi, Bart Starr, and Frank Gifford personalized the participants.

"We began making the game personal for the fans, like a Hollywood movie," Sabol told The Associated Press in 2011. "Violent tackles, the long slow spiral of the ball, following alongside the players as they sidestepped and sprinted down the field, the movie camera was the perfect medium at the time to present the game the way the fans wanted to see it."

Not only see it, but feel it. The Sabols understood long before reality television stormed the tube that sports were the true reality TV. While the players—at various times referred to as gladiators, warriors, and, yes pirates—and their achievements were often glorified by NFL Films, the foundation of the presentations was the action. More accurately, getting inside the action.

"We see the game as art as much as sport," Steve Sabol said. "That helped us nurture not only the game's traditions but to develop its mythology: 'America's Team,' 'The Catch,' 'The Frozen Tundra.'"

Also helping develop that mythology were the voices who followed Facenda, including regular narrators Jeff Kaye and Harry Kalas, and an assortment of celebrities who reached out to the Sabols to take part: Orson Welles, Burt Lancaster, Charlton Heston, Gene Hackman, Bruce Willis, Vincent Price, Ed Harris, Martin Sheen, and Donald Sutherland.

"The creation of NFL Films in the early 1960s no doubt played a significant role in the growth of popularity of the National Football League," a Hall of Fame statement said when Ed Sabol was elected as a contributor. "NFL Films has revolutionized the manner in which sports are presented on camera."

And even with the Sabols gone, it is still a game changer.

SHORT LIST

Five Great Titles from the *NFL Films Presents* Television Series

NFL FILMS PRESENTS—1985, SHOW #9
TITLE: Ugliest Uniforms, Roger Staubach, Tony Dorsett

NFL FILMS PRESENTS—1986, SHOW #11
TITLE: Tight End, the Strippers, 1950 NY Giants Defense

NFL FILMS PRESENTS—1995, SHOW #3
TITLE: Summer Camp Torture (Summer Harvest, A Journeyman's Ride, 49ers Family)

NFL FILMS PRESENTS—1996, SHOW #8
TITLE: Connie Gomper (Fictional character telling real-life stories about Packer fans)

NFL FILMS PRESENTS—1998, SHOW #10
TITLE: The Dullest Show Ever, Glanville, History of Get Back Coach, Dullest Plays, Coaches Conversation

Artificial Turf

The Carpet Causes Much Worse than Rug Burns

Wendell Davis was a solid NFL wide receiver. No record-setter by any means, but a signficant contributor for the Chicago Bears. Then Davis established an unenviable mark in sports, tearing up *both* knees on the same play.

At fault? Not an opponent targeting his limbs and ravaging them with a monstrous tackle. Not some obstacle, like a goalpost stanchion or a sideline post. To blame, without doubt, was the carpet at Veterans Stadium in Philadelphia.

Already considered the worst artificial turf in the league—and probably for any outdoor sport—the Vet rug had no mercy. Davis started going up for a reception and heard something snap. He fell to the ground as the football flew past him. The pain was immeasurable—times two.

NO.

Davis considered legal action, but "after looking into it, we found it would be very hard . . . to prove that a spot on the field caused my injury."

For decades, though, the carpets developed in the 1960s by such industrial giants as Monsanto—its AstroTurf creation was so popular that the backyard in *The Brady Bunch* television show had AstroTurf instead of real grass—were so in vogue that many newer stadiums planned to use them from Day One. The most famous play in NFL history, the Immaculate Reception, occurred on the Three Rivers Stadium rug in 1972, for example. That came eight years after ChemGrass was invented by Monsanto, although not for any professional teams but for a private school. It was not until baseball's Houston Astros discovered that the type of natural grass they were using at the Astrodome couldn't survive—semi-transparent ceiling panels blocked sunlight—that the fake stuff made its way to professional sports.

There's nothing natural about Boise State's blue turf.

On a Disastrous Injury Caused by Artificial Turf

"I basically saw that I had no kneecaps." —*Wendell Davis to the* Philadelphia Inquirer *about the 1993 injury that would end his career*

AUDIBLE

It was renamed in 1966 to AstroTurf by Monsanto employee John A. Wortmann. The Houston Oilers began playing on it two years later at the stadium. And when other pro franchises saw the financial (if not aesthetic) benefits of rug over real, they began following suit—particularly those teams in the NFL, where fields got torn up so badly that little grass remained by mid-November. Owners loved the idea from the beginning: Put down the rug, clean it (imagine the size of those vacuums!), and kick off the next game on the patch of phony green glued to the concrete or cement or whatever was below.

While those owners were thrilled they didn't have the headaches of dirt fields instead of grass for two months of the season, or didn't have to replant the real stuff, the players pretty much loathed the synthetics. Forget that it often favored skill position guys who could run faster and cut sharper on the better carpets, something even Davis acknowledged. Unfortunately, there were very few of those better carpets, and the seams needed to join together portions of the rugs seemed to have a Loch Ness monster underneath, grabbing feet, making them stick in the turf. Voila: wrecked knees, broken ankles, torn muscles.

The players' union sensed the dangers as far back as 1973, when it sought a moratorium on the installation of synthetic turf. But several studies back then could find no overwhelming proof that the rugs were more dangerous for players. In inclement weather, the carpets often provided more consistent footing, and it was easier to remove ice and snow from it than from grass.

So to judge the impact of artificial turf on football solely by Davis's misfortune or by Joe Namath's alleged quip that he couldn't compare AstroTurf to grass because he'd never smoked AstroTurf would be unfair, experts say.

"It's been a love-hate relationship," Andrew McNitt, professor of soil science and director of the Center for Sports Surface Research at Penn State, told *Sports Illustrated*. "There is a traditionalist in all of us that really wants to see games played on natural grass. But in 1970, the state of the art and science of growing natural grass was way behind where it is today. Along came artificial turf. Coaches raved about how great it was. Then there was criticism."

That criticism of all brands of synthetic surfaces—Tartan Turf, PolyTurf, SuperTurf, All-Pro and the likes—centered on the ugly injuries, and even the smaller ones such as rug burns that turned skin into raw, ugly, and painful messes.

It also focused on the cement-like hardness of the artificial turf. Hall of Fame tackle Dan Dierdorf said decades after his retirement that ailments he suffered later in life stemmed from so many practices and games on carpets. "I sometimes sit and think about how different my life would be right now if I had been drafted by the Raiders or the Chargers," Dierdorf told *Sports Illustrated*, mentioning teams that always have used natural grass fields in their stadiums. "I wouldn't be the cripple that I am now. I'm not feeling sorry for myself, and I'm not blaming anyone. I just wish it was different. The Cardinals didn't say, 'Let's put this artificial turf in so we can cripple our players.' For a little while, the league had a love affair with artificial turf. Who knew what was happening? Nobody knew."

Eventually, along came the modern faux grass: vastly improved, safer, much more like true grass, and still easy to maintain.

"Then there was a lot of positive talk with the development of the (current) artificial turf, and now a little bit of criticism again," McNitt said. "Now we can sod a field and play on it the next day. That was not the case in the 1970s."

For the purists, there always will be a contentious relationship with artificial turf—at least until someone develops something synthetic that has all the positive attributes of grass and none of the ills of the ersatz stuff.

Eventually, along came the modern faux grass: vastly improved, safer, much more like true grass, and still easy to maintain.

The College Conference Conga

The Big Ten, Big 12, and SEC Ain't What They Used to Be

Being a college football fan used to be so simple.

The Big Ten had 10 teams, naturally. The Big 12 had a dozen. ACC teams were situated somewhere near the Atlantic Coast. Same for the Pacific-8/10 and its ocean. Notre Dame, Army, and Navy were the major independents.

Everything made sense.

Then the College Conference Conga began, blowing up the landscape from Syracuse (once a Big East power, now a minnow in the ACC) to Colorado (located in Boulder, 1,000 miles from the Pacific Ocean, yet a Pac-12 member these days).

There's so much more: Big 8/10/12 mainstay Nebraska now sits in the Big Ten. The Southeastern Conference—that's *Southeastern*—has ignored all geographical logic by adding Texas A&M and Missouri.

Even the smaller conferences have gone haywire: among the Sun Belt teams are Idaho and New Mexico State. UMass and Buffalo are in the Mid-American.

Notre Dame, of South Bend, Indiana, has joined the ACC, sort of, although it still has its own network, NBC, to telecast all of the Irish's home games. While joining the ACC, Notre Dame still maintained its status as a football independent.

Thankfully, all 13 teams in Conference USA reside in the good old US of A.

Alabama and the Southeastern Conference invited
Texas A&M and Missouri to their dance.

SHORT LIST

2016 Football Division 1-A Conferences

Atlantic Coast (ACC)

Big 12

Big Ten

Pac-12

Southeastern (SEC)

American Athletic Conference (AAC)

Conference USA

Mid-American (MAC)

Mountain West

Sun Belt

Western Athletic (WAC)

Independent FBS Teams

"Change is never easy. But I think over time people will accept it, and everything will level and even out," former Minnesota athletic director Joel Maturi told The Associated Press in 2014.

There are millions, even billions of reasons (read: dollars) for the seismic shifts.

No, it's not the $outheastern Conference. Not yet. But as long as CB$ and E$PN are paying hand over fist to televise and webcast conference games, a sense of stability is impossible.

The college football map began to change in 1990, but only slightly, when eastern powerhouse Penn State joined the Big Ten. There was enough logic to the move because the Nittany Lions weren't ridiculously far from some conference members, and they recruited in similar areas.

Still, the Big Ten then had 11 teams; of course, as of 2016 it was up to 14.

In 1992, the earth began shaking a whole lot more. Arkansas, a longtime Southwest Conference mainstay, headed to the SEC, as did independent South Carolina. By increasing its enrollment to 12 teams, the SEC could split into two divisions of six schools and stage a conference championship game between the division winners. A game worth, well, millions.

The SEC's financial success in the 90s preceded its on-field domination in the 2000s, but the league had set in motion a game-changing approach that lasted two decades.

The machinations included teams from the East, West, North, South, and Central regions moving up to Division I, which became the Football Bowl Subdivision (FBS), and joining established or new conferences. Mostly, though, the maneuvering focused on big-time schools who could bring prestige, fans, TV interest, and, ah yes, money to the table.

When the Southwest Conference disappeared in 1996, ending 82 years of life, it pretty much was soaked up by the Big Eight to form the Big 12. Texas, Texas A&M, Texas Tech, and Baylor moved to the Big 12 to join Oklahoma and Oklahoma State in the South Division. Nebraska, Colorado, Missouri, Kansas, Kansas State, and Iowa State formed the North.

In basketball country, also known as the ACC, Florida State had come aboard in 1991, but the status quo would not be disturbed much until the next decade. That same year, another basketball-dominated league, the Big East, went big on football, too. It enticed such major programs as Miami, West Virginia, and Virginia Tech to join, along with Rutgers and Temple. The one school the Big East really had wanted, Penn State, had gone to the Big Ten the previous year, embittering many of the Big East universities, particularly Pitt and Syracuse.

After all that spinning, the wheels on the college football affiliation buses stopped going round and round until 2004. Then, everything began to blow up.

"To strive and thrive, you've got to get bigger. Conference realignment is about exactly that: having more economic value when you get bigger," sports media consultant Chris Bevilacqua told The Associated Press.

The most recent tidal waves, spread over a 10-year period, fashioned the following:

In 2004, Miami and Virginia Tech left the Big East for the ACC, and Temple was ejected from the league for not carrying enough weight as a football program. Boston College followed that route the next year, prompting the Big East to reach out to Cincinnati, Louisville, and South Florida.

The key move came in 2010 when Nebraska applied for Big Ten membership. The Cornhuskers joined the league in 2011—giving the Big Ten a total of 12 teams and allowing it to split into two sectors and stage a title game.

Also in 2011, Utah (Mountain West) and Colorado (Big 12) headed to the Pac-10, and as the Pac-12, the conference could hold a championship match.

Meanwhile, the ACC grabbed Syracuse and Pitt from the Big East.

Missouri and Texas A&M made their big moves in 2012, leaving the Big 12 for the SEC. The Big 12 countered by grabbing West Virginia away from the Big East and signing up TCU, which had an agreement to go to the Big East but never actually did. What exactly is Texas Christian, located in Fort Worth, east of anyway?

Those defections forced the Big East to invite back Temple and, the next season, to ask Central Florida, Houston, SMU, Boise State, and San Diego State to come aboard. Yes—four schools from way west of the Mississippi River. Houston, SMU, and UCF among them wound up in the reincarnation of the Big East, the American Athletic Conference.

The dizziness-provoking moves slowed down after 2014, the year that Maryland hightailed it from the ACC to the Big Ten, and Rutgers also joined that conference. The idea of getting the New York, Baltimore, and Washington, DC, markets into the Big Ten's lair was too rewarding to pass up.

Is it over? Not a chance.

The idea of getting the New York, Baltimore, and Washington, DC, markets into the Big Ten's lair was too rewarding to pass up.

Amos Alonzo Stagg

The Innovator Who Was There from (Before) the Beginning

NO. 24

Amos Alonzo Stagg, the legendary football coach, was not ready to retire at 70. The University of Chicago disagreed. So in 1933 Stagg went looking for another job.

Taking Horace Greeley's advice to "Go west, young man," he found it. Out west he coached at the College of the Pacific in Stockton, California, until 1946, when he was 83. He still wasn't ready to retire.

From 1947 to 1952, he coached at Susquehanna University in Pennsylvania, sharing coaching duties with his son. At 90, he went back to California for a few more years as an advisory coach. He retired at the age of 98 in 1960.

Stagg is not only known for his longevity but for the influence he had on both football and basketball, having been inducted into both Halls of Fame.

Stagg introduced or helped develop many of the innovations in football we have today. They included the principles of the modern T-formation that led to Knute Rockne's spectacular success at Notre Dame, and the Single Wing that Pop Warner developed at many schools. Stagg is also credited—in some cases erroneously—with inventing the huddle, the center snap, the forward pass, the end-around, and the tackling dummy among many others too numerous to list.

Stagg was born in West Orange, New Jersey, in 1862 before the invention of football. As a four-year-old standing on a street corner in West Orange, Stagg remembered waving a Union flag welcoming home Civil War soldiers. His family was poor, but Stagg wanted to go to Yale. He saved and worked hard, so at 22 he was able to enroll as a Divinity student.

Amos Alonzo Stagg off the field and standing on top of the sideline with his 1901 Chicago Maroons

On Playing for Amos Alonzo Stagg

"If he was upset with you, he'd call you a jackass. If he was really upset, he'd call you a double jackass. And about once in a season, when he was really hot, he'd call somebody a triple jackass." —*Al Lewis, former player for Stagg at Pacific*

AUDIBLE

Tuition was $50, but only $30 for Divinity students. The tuition left little for food, and he was starving until he found a job waiting tables at the student dining hall. Regaining robust health, his athletic career took off.

Stagg was widely regarded as the best amateur pitcher in the country. In an Ivy League game he once struck out 20 Princeton batters. Because of a deep belief in amateurism, Stagg once rejected a $4,200 offer to play the last three months of a season for the New York Giants. Proclaimed a headline in the *New Haven Register*: YALE IS HAPPY. GREAT STAGG PROMISES TO PITCH FOR HER AGAIN.

As a graduate student at Yale's Divinity school, he started playing football in 1888. With Stagg in the lineup, Yale went 14-0 and 15-1 over two seasons. His performance earned him a spot as an end on Walter Camp's first All-America team.

Stagg, meanwhile, had second thoughts about his career as a preacher. He realized he stammered too much and was uncomfortable as a public speaker. He made a decision: an athletic career for him.

In 1890, he began his career coaching football at the Springfield (Mass.) YMCA, now Springfield College. One of his players, James Naismith, invented basketball one year later. The first public basketball game was held at the Springfield "Y." Stagg scored the only basket in a 5–1 loss to the students at a time when a basket only counted one point. He introduced the sport to the University of Chicago, where he developed the five-on-five format.

But it was football where Stagg made his biggest impact, and at a time when the sport was in trouble, in the early 1900s. The fields in America were littered with broken bodies, and on too many occasions, dead bodies.

Stagg was among several of the nation's top college coaches summoned to the White House by President Theodore Roosevelt in 1906 to help save the sport. Out of the meeting came new rules with the object of making football safer, most notably the legalization of the forward pass. A story in the *New York Times* reported that Stagg devised no less than 64 pass plays.

At the University of Chicago his teams won two National Championships and seven Big Ten titles in one of the toughest conferences in the country.

At the University of Chicago his teams won two National Championships and seven Big Ten titles in one of the toughest conferences in the country.

In 1932 at the age of 70, Stagg brought his Chicago team to Yale as underdogs. Stagg's team managed a 7–7 tie.

After the season, the university thought he was too old to coach. Stagg thought differently—after all, he had only been coaching football for 40 years. Still much too young to retire, he thought.

So he accepted the coaching position at the College of the Pacific. "I'm as happy about my decision as a college sophomore with his first varsity football letter," Stagg said. "Naturally a big lump comes up into my throat when I think of leaving all my friends behind, but I'm too young, too active to give up coaching."

On the way to California, President Herbert Hoover was on the same train as Stagg. A large crowd greeted the train when it arrived in Stockton. Stagg was sure the crowd was there only to see Hoover. Not so. Stagg was also greeted with a great reception.

Even though he had come from a large school in the East, he never complained about anything in California. "He was the most tolerant individual I've ever known," said Pacific athletic director Bob Breedon.

Stagg's 1939 Pacific team, when Stagg was 77, beat Chicago 39–0, turning the tables on the team Stagg once coached. Stagg wasn't too old then, huh?

Stagg remained at the University of Pacific for 13 seasons until he was forced to retire for a second time. Once again, he unretired himself and continued to coach at Susquehanna, sharing duties with his son, Lonnie.

Stagg continued to keep his hand in football in an advisory capacity. He remained strong past his 101st birthday, then passed away.

Knute Rockne gave Stagg the ultimate tribute. When asked about Stagg's contribution to football, Rockne said: "All football comes from Stagg."

Paul Brown

The Innovator Who Put the "Modern" in the Modern Game

The intelligence test. The playbook. The use of film clips. Taxi squads. These are a few of Paul Brown's many innovations.

He was a winner at every level: high school, college, the military, and the professional leagues. According to one source, Brown won 351 games, or 70 percent of his coaching starts. And he made an immediate impact once he stepped on a football field as a coach.

At Massillon (Ohio) High School in the 1930s—considered the cradle of football coaching—his team lost only one of 60 games. It was a football-mad community and brought Coach Brown national attention.

In 1941 Brown became the coach at Ohio State. One year later he coached the Buckeyes to the unofficial national championship.

When the United States went to war, Brown became a Navy lieutenant. He was told to put together a football team at the Great Lakes Naval Training Center in Illinois.

"The admiral told me it was good for morale," Brown said.

He had total freedom to choose his players. "I was told to be on the alert for anyone coming through," Brown said. "I had coached in the Big Ten so anyone coming through, I had their folders pulled out. We held them over and tested them."

He put together a team that was one of the most powerful in the United States.

When the war was over, Brown was heading to a new team in Cleveland and a new league: the All American Football Conference (AAFC). After a fan vote, owner Mickey McBride decided to call his new team the Browns after Paul Brown, even though the coach didn't like it. In an alternate version, the club media guide linked the team name to fighter Joe Louis, nicknamed The Brown Bomber.

NO. 25

Cleveland Browns head coach Paul Brown, August 25, 1961

On the Impact of a Brilliant Coach

"Whether they know it or not, nearly everyone in the game of football has been affected by Paul Brown. His wealth of ideas changed the game." —*former NFL commissioner Pete Rozelle*

AUDIBLE

Brown went to work doing things differently. He had intelligence tests for players, and a year-round coaching staff diagramming patterns for his receivers and sending in plays by messenger guard, a practice used for many years.

The Browns were an immediate success, winning four straight titles in the AAFC. They posted 47 victories, 4 losses, and 3 ties in that time.

Still, there was some skepticism when the Browns joined the NFL in 1950. Could they keep up with the established NFL teams that ruled pro football? Well, the Browns made believers of the skeptics, winning an NFL title in their very first season in the league. Then they won league championships under Brown in 1954 and 1955.

The Browns continued to roll, winning another NFL title in 1964, although by that time Coach Brown had been fired by owner Art Modell.

"For the first 10 years we were in the championship game," Groza said. "We didn't always win it, but we were in it. [Brown] used to relate to us that he thought of us as the New York Yankees of football."

Brown was known as a no-nonsense coach. When his team had a 29-game winning streak stopped in 1949, he called his players together. They expected praise for their streak, but this is what Brown had to say: "I'm telling you this and it's cold turkey. If those of you who fell down on the job don't bounce back, I'll sell you."

In the 1950s Brown decided to try electronic innovation in his messenger system. Standing with a walkie-talkie on the sideline, Brown had installed a receiver in quarterback George Ratterman's helmet. The problem: radio interference, including police calls. It made it difficult to hear the football talk.

One afternoon at Yankee Stadium, Ratterman called time out, pulled off his helmet, and approached Brown. Visibly upset, he said: "Coach, some guy just got stabbed over on Fifth Avenue."

Brown put a particular emphasis on the extensive use of game films. Players would live in terrible fear of Brown's Monday morning quarterback sessions.

"I remember Dub Jones scored five touchdowns against Chicago and the next day Paul didn't find anything right with him," Motley told The Associated Press. "He would pick out one guy and show every little thing he did wrong."

Brown always made sure his message got through to his players. From Day One, Brown warned them: no T-shirts in training camp, no smoking in front of children, and no drinking in public during the season.

Standing with a walkie-talkie on the sideline, Brown had installed a receiver in quarterback George Ratterman's helmet.

Brown, meanwhile, was usually the best-dressed coach on the field. "I was probably the first coach to dress up," he said. He could be seen roaming the sideline wearing his signature hat, a knotted tie, looking very debonair.

Times changed and the new owner, Modell, dismissed the 54-year-old Brown in 1963. He was free to travel, play golf, but he was miserable.

"I had everything a man can want: leisure, enough money, a wonderful family. Yet with all that, I was eating my heart out," said Brown. "Football has been my life. I had a strong desire to become alive again."

And so he did, founding his second franchise in the NFL in 1967: the Cincinnati Bengals. He built the Bengals into a strong team, winning division championships in 1970, 1973, and 1975. After the 1975 season, he resigned as head coach. But he continued as vice president and general manager, loving football and never wanting to leave.

"He was the best that ever was," said Lin Huston, who played for Brown at Massillon High School, at Ohio State, and then for the Browns from 1946 to 1953. "He left nothing to chance. He was detail oriented and wouldn't assume anything. He'd say, 'OK, Let's see you do it.'"

Brown's disciples of Super Bowl success are spread across the map of the National Football League: Chuck Noll won four in Pittsburgh, Bill Walsh three with San Francisco, and Don Shula two with Miami. In addition, Weeb Ewbank (New York Jets) and Don McCafferty (Baltimore) also each won a Super Bowl to bring the total of Super Bowl winners linked to Brown to 11. All have been thankful to Brown for leading the way.

"Do you want to call it a miniature war?" Brown asked one day. "Or chess in hip pads? Whatever. Football is absorbing, exciting, intriguing. It's a man's life."

And an extraordinary life it was.

The Fighting Irish

Knute Rockne, Grantland Rice, and "Win One for the Gipper"

NO. 26

Notre Dame's star pass catcher was nervous. The Irish were unveiling a new game plan in 1913 and Knute Rockne would be a very large part of it.

A rule change that would become effective that fall removed all restrictions on the length of a legal forward pass. Rockne and quarterback Gus Dorais were preparing to take advantage.

It had all started when Rockne and Dorais practiced running and catching on the beach, throwing the ball at all angles in the summer of 1913. People who didn't know they were preparing for their final football season "probably thought we were crazy," Rockne said. Dorais invented a better way to throw the ball that summer and Rockne developed a better way to catch it.

When the Irish slaughtered the powerful Army team in 1913, Rockne's big moment had come. The historic contest was played on November 1, and the Cadets expected it to be a "breather." It was, for a while. And even though the Cadets were caught short by Notre Dame's passing game, they still managed to hold a 14–13 halftime lead. Then in the second half, Dorais said, "Let's open up," remembered Rockne. The Irish unleashed a passing attack featuring Rockne and Gus Dorais that no one had ever seen before in the East.

Footballs filled the air as Dorais connected with Rockne on several high-flying plays. Dorais threw an unheard-of volume of passes in those days, 17. Bill Roper, the former head coach at Princeton, said he knew such play was possible under the new rules, but that he had never seen the forward pass developed to such a state of perfection. Some of the passes traveled 35 to 40 yards to the receivers, a nearly miraculous distance in those days.

Notre Dame's "Four Horsemen of the Apocalypse" backfield (1924) and Knute Rockne

SHORT LIST

Notre Dame Consensus National Championship Seasons

1924, 1929, 1930, 1943, 1946, 1947, 1949, 1966, 1973, 1977, 1988

The school does not officially recognize the 1938 and 1953 National Championships.

The Fighting Irish handed the Cadets a sound beating, 35–13, and received a hero's welcome back home.

And how about Rockne on the sidelines? From 1918 to 1930 no football coach was more revered than Rockne, who turned the small midwestern school of Notre Dame into a national power with his innovative plays and inspirational salesmanship.

As Notre Dame coach, another important moment for Rockne came on October 19, 1924. Fans woke up to read in the sports pages about the Four Horsemen of Notre Dame. Legendary sportswriter Grantland Rice's lead story in the *New York Herald Tribune* soon became part of the Notre Dame lore. After Notre Dame beat another great Army team, Rice filed this lead in the *Tribune*:

"Outlined against a blue-gray October sky, the Four Horsemen rode again. In dramatic lore they are known as Famine, Pestilence, Destruction and Death. These are only aliases. Their real names are Stuhldreher, Miller, Crowley and Layden.

"They formed the crest of the South Bend cyclone before which another fighting Army football team was swept over the precipice at the Polo Grounds yesterday afternoon . . ."

The Four Horsemen, playing in the deceptive Notre Dame Shift, featured Jim Crowley, Harry Stuhldreher, Elmer Layden, and Don Miller. They became arguably the most famous backfield in football history, and considerably raised Notre Dame's image in the football world.

The Irish returned home from the game and Crowley recalled: "The reason why we were remembered was because of the name Granny Rice gave us, plus the fact that when we got back to South Bend, a student athletic public relations man (George Strickland, later sports editor of the *Chicago Tribune*) got four horses out there and they put us on the horses. The picture went out all over the country. The fact is, people got curious about us and that was in mid-October. Then we went out to win every game after that and played in the Rose Bowl, and won that game. But I think if we had lost a game or two after that splurge of Granny Rice and the picture, I don't think we would have been remembered."

Crowley said that the Four Horsemen "were much smaller, but we were just as fast [as other backfields]. Our main forte for the day was speed and deception."

"Layden was a track man. He held track records in high school in Iowa," Crowley added. "Don Miller was a track man, and I had good football speed. I could change direction without losing any normal speed."

Another special moment for Notre Dame: the Gipper game.

In 1928 the Irish faced Army at Yankee Stadium in another of their classic confrontations. This time the Irish were struggling and were underdogs to a deep Army team that featured a host of All-Americans, including the great Chris Cagle.

Rockne was having the worst time of his coaching career. He had lost two games and a third seemed a certainty against a powerful Army team.

So what did Rockne do? Only come up with the most dramatic locker room speech in college football history. Rockne was an excellent motivator, and sometimes his stories were even true.

So what did Rockne do? Only come up with the most dramatic locker room speech in college football history.

Rockne recalled standing beside the deathbed of George Gipp. He listened to the dying athlete say, "Coach, when the going gets rough, especially against Army, win one for me." Rockne emphasized it was important not only to them, the boys themselves, but to answer the prayer of the Gipper, who was a convert to Catholicism on his deathbed. Line coach Ed Healy remembered, "There was no one that wasn't crying, including Rockne and me. There was a moment of silence, and then all of a sudden those players ran out of the dressing room and almost tore the hinges off the door. They were all ready to kill someone."

There was no stopping the Irish after that. They raced onto the field and won the game, 12–6. The game was recounted in a movie, *Knute Rockne, All-American*, featuring Ronald Reagan in the role of the Gipper. The movie kept the legend alive.

In his time at Notre Dame, Rockne posted an unmatched record: 105 wins, only 12 losses, and five ties for a winning percentage of .897. Five of his teams had unbeaten, untied records, and three won National Championships.

Rockne's life was cut short by a plane crash in 1930. The Notre Dame stadium, clearly the House That Rockne Built, was finished the same year. Unfortunately, Rockne never saw its completion.

1970 Alabama vs. Southern Cal

The All-White Crimson Tide Host the Integrated Trojans

NO. **27**

The phone rang in the office of John McKay, the Southern Cal football coach. It was Alabama coach Bear Bryant calling. He wanted to set up a game with the Trojans.

An NCAA rules change enabled colleges to schedule an extra game for the 1970 season. So Bryant suggested to his good friend that their teams meet in the opening game, even though the Crimson Tide were deep underdogs to the Trojans.

The Southern Cal team reigned as the powerhouse of the West:

- Four straight Rose Bowl appearances;
- Two recent Heisman Trophy winners, Mike Garrett and O. J. Simpson;
- A 21-game regular-season victory streak.

Alabama, meanwhile, hadn't won a championship since 1965 and had been struggling of late. McKay didn't want to embarrass his friend.

"I thought it would be a bad idea," McKay said, "because I thought we would beat them."

McKay finally decided to set up a home-and-home series with Alabama, starting with the opener in Tuscaloosa in 1970. Once the game was arranged, McKay broke the news to his players at spring practice.

Southern California Trojans quarterback Jimmy Jones, November 22, 1969

On the Outcome of the 1970 USC-Alabama Game

"The point of the game was never the score. The point of the game was reason, democracy and hope. The real winner that night was the South." —Los Angeles Times *columnist Jim Murray*

AUDIBLE

One of them, African-American defensive end Tody Smith, reportedly went out and bought a gun. "He got it for self-protection," said John Papadakis, then the Trojans' starting middle linebacker. "He's from Texas and had seen some things."

With racial issues tearing apart the country, it was a time of violence and change in America. Even though President Lyndon Johnson had signed the civil rights bill in the mid-1960s, there were still large pockets of resistance to integration, particularly in the Deep South.

As late as 1970, the Alabama football team was completely white, while Southern Cal featured a number of talented black players, including its entire backfield.

"I don't recall us making a big issue, though we had some concerns about our safety," said Southern Cal quarterback Jimmy Jones. "We were aware that we were the first integrated team to play them at their place. It was added incentive for us, as I'm sure it was added incentive for them. We knew the history of the South. It meant a lot for us to be successful."

The Southern Cal football team was walking into a region with a bitter history of racial trouble. In the summer of 1963, Alabama governor George Wallace made a defiant "stand at the schoolhouse door," literally shutting the door on black students attempting to enroll at Alabama. Wallace's position on segregation was brutally clear. In one of his inaugural addresses (Wallace served several terms as Alabama governor), he had uttered his infamous words: "Segregation now, segregation tomorrow, segregation forever."

That same year, four young African-American girls were killed when their church was bombed. In Jackson, Mississippi, civil rights leader Medgar Evers was assassinated. Use African-American players on Alabama's football team? Not likely at this point.

"The political climate in the state wasn't right," said Glenn Gryska, a former assistant under Bryant.

But times were changing, thanks to the surging civil rights movement in America. By 1970, Bryant had indeed recruited his first black player, wide receiver Wilbur Jackson. Bryant had sent assistant coach Pat Dye to Ozark, Alabama, to offer Jackson a scholarship.

By the 1970 season opener against Southern Cal on September 12, Jackson was sitting in the stands at Legion Field in Birmingham along with 72,174 others. His start on Alabama's football team would have to wait a year; at the time the NCAA did not allow freshmen to play.

Although Alabama and Southern Cal had two of the top football programs in the nation, they hadn't met in 25 years. The Trojans had won that 1945 Rose Bowl game, 34–14.

The 1970 game started—and revealed just how lacking the Crimson Tide was.

"When they came up to the line to play us man to man, we thought it was going to be a piece of cake," Gryska said. "But they covered us like a blanket. Inevitably, we had to get better athletes."

Southern Cal dominated the game from start to finish.

"We were treated respectfully," Jones said. "No one in the stands said anything overtly racist—it was more of a gawking kind of thing. On the field, I think a couple of linemen heard the N-word in the heat of the game, but they were isolated incidents."

Sam "Bam" Cunningham, a 6-foot-3, 215-pound sophomore running back, set the tone for the day when he scored on runs of 22 and 4 yards in the first half. The Trojans took a 22–7 lead at the half and expanded it to 32–7 in the third quarter.

According to one sportswriter, Cunningham "scattered tacklers around like confetti." By the time the game was over, Cunningham had piled up 135 yards.

Clarence Davis, an Alabama native whose family had fled the South, rushed for 76 yards and scored on a 23-yard pass from Jones. Every USC touchdown was scored by a black player.

Final: Southern Cal 42, Alabama 21.

Every USC touchdown was scored by a black player. Final: Southern Cal 42, Alabama 21.

The outcome of the game brought about change. Bryant pushed his university for black recruitment and athletic scholarships. "Kids who either had to go to the Black colleges, Midwest or out West, could now get a chance to play not far from home from the areas where they grew up," said Cunningham.

Soon Alabama would have an increasingly large number of black players. In 1970 Alabama went 6-5-1; in 1971, the Tide went 11-1 and won more games than any football team of the decade. They were on the way to three National Championships.

When the Tide went undefeated in 1979, there were 16 African Americans starting for Alabama.

Broadway Joe

Namath Takes Over the Entire Football World

He came to New York as a Western Pennsylvania kid by way of Alabama.

Before he ever took the field, he was the richest rookie in pro football. Soon, he was as popular in the Big Apple as Mantle and Berra—even Sinatra.

A few years later, Broadway Joe Namath wouldn't just own Manhattan and the other boroughs; he'd own the entire football world.

Guaranteed!

"I had no idea when I came to the Jets that all of that would happen," Namath said, flashing that grin that charmed coeds and matrons alike, "but I am sure glad it did."

NO. 28

"All of that" began when Sonny Werblin, whose background was in entertainment, bought the relatively dormant New York Titans and renamed them the Jets, plunking the AFL team in the new Shea Stadium hard by LaGuardia Airport. Werblin knew his franchise could never compete with the established Giants of the NFL without some star power.

Enter Namath in 1965 as the Jets outbid the NFL's Cardinals for the quarterback Crimson Tide coach Bear Bryant once said would be "pretty good." So good—at least at the box office and as a marketing tool—that Werblin paid Namath the outrageous sum of $400,000. "I believe it is the largest amount ever given to an athlete for professional services," Werblin bragged.

That was the first time Namath changed the pro game; from then forevermore, quarterbacks would command top dollar even if they hadn't proven themselves.

And while Namath's deal hardly was the first salvo in the bidding wars between the AFL and NFL, it was the loudest, and hastened to bring the sides together because owners were fearful of escalating salaries.

Broadway Joe Namath still had it on in 2014 at Super Bowl XLVIII.

SHORT LIST

Products Endorsed by Broadway Joe

* Popcorn * Hot Cocoa

* Cologne * Deodorant

* Boots * Shoes * Underwear

* Shaving Cream * Pantyhose

* and More

Though Namath wasn't an instant star in the AFL—New York didn't make the playoffs until 1968 with him behind center—his impact in the media was immediate. Few sports stars had been the centerpiece of as many promotional and advertising campaigns, but the TV cameras loved Namath. So did the folks watching what those cameras brought into their living rooms and into the taverns, including Bachelors III, an ill-fated bar Namath briefly owned and was forced to sell by Commissioner Pete Rozelle.

Joe Willie didn't just pitch footballs. He pitched popcorn, hot cocoa, cologne, and more.

Game changer No. 2.

The public loved it. So did his teammates.

"He helped us get a contract with Puma," Jets star linebacker Larry Grantham said. "We were on TV and they would pay us to wear these shoes. It was because of Joe. We were still out there to make a living."

It wasn't just the Jets that Namath was helping popularize. Throughout the AFL and NFL in the 1960s, as pro football began its unimpeded rise to America's favorite sport, players from both leagues were following in his wake. Lance Alworth became a receiving icon, playing off his "Bambi" nickname and super route running. Dick Butkus was the ballcarrier-breaking middle linebacker who could run through blockers and walls. Johnny Unitas not only wore high tops as he worked his passing magic, but he, too, would be paid to wear them.

At the same time, Namath was earning another nickname for wearing white shoes on the field: Joe Willie White Shoes—of course. And don't forget the full-length fur coats he sported in deep winter, usually with a beautiful starlet—or two—on his arm.

For all of that, Namath's heftiest impact came in South Florida in January 1969. Some folks still argue that his words, actions, and persona in those few days leading to Super Bowl III did more to legitimize the AFL than anything else in the 10-season history of the league.

The first two meetings of the NFL and AFL champions resulted in victories for the Vince Lombardi–led Green Bay Packers. They were one-sided enough that the younger league was being dismissed as interlopers. This merger thing was a joke to fans of the established league, who believed no AFL team belonged on the same field with their Packers and Giants and Browns and Colts.

Especially the Colts, who stormed into the Super Bowl as 19-point favorites over the Jets. Baltimore had manhandled Cleveland 34–0 to earn its place opposite Namath's motley bunch.

Then Namath enraged the Colts and their followers three days before the game at the Miami Touchdown Club luncheon when he was honored as the Pro Football Player of the Year.

As he stepped to the podium, a Colts fan in the audience yelled: "Hey, Namath, we're going to kick your ass."

His wit as quick as his arm was strong, Namath replied: "I've got news for you. We're going to win the game. I guarantee it."

The only person more ticked by Namath's proclamation than the Colts had to be Jets coach Weeb Ewbank. Namath later admitted Ewbank asked him if he "was crazy."

Crazy as a fox. And on Super Sunday, brilliantly using his running game led by fullback Matt Snell (30 carries, 121 yards, one TD), mixing in passes to George Sauer (eight catches, 133 yards), supported by the field goals of Jim Turner and a staunch, big-play defense, Namath did the impossible.

Jets 16, Colts 7.

"The guarantee probably was one of the greatest things Joe could have done," his center, John Schmitt, said proudly. "The Colts were really pissed off. They wanted to kill Joe and kill us."

Instead, they were humbled. So were their fans—all NFL fans, for that matter. Team owners, too.

The AFL? No longer was it the little kid that the big bully could knock around at will.

The AFL? No longer was it the little kid that the big bully could knock around at will.

For good measure, the Kansas City Chiefs, admittedly inspired by what the Jets had done to the Colts, eased past another supposedly unbeatable NFL representative in the big game, the Minnesota Vikings, in Super Bowl IV the following year. As the full merger took place, the Super Bowl ledger stood NFL 2, AFL 2.

Equal partners.

Thank you, Broadway Joe.

The 1982 NFL Strike

Labor of Non-Love

If baseball could do it, so could football.

After major league baseball players staged their 50-day, 712-game job action in 1981 over free agency compensation, the NFL guys walked out the following year. While it was the fourth labor dispute between the football players and team owners—the other three were lockouts or strikes during the offseason or preseason—it was the first to affect the regular season.

Did it ever: 57 days, costing the schedule seven games per team. The issues were revenue sharing, minimum salaries, preseason and postseason pay, medical insurance, retirement benefits, and severance pay.

NO. 29

Which side won? Depends on your allegiances, but management did not have to give in on establishing free agency, which would not truly hit the NFL for another 11 years. Ed Garvey, the executive director of the union, instead pushed for 55 percent of the NFL's gross revenues because, among other reasons, Garvey detested player agents and didn't want them having the power that would come with free agency.

Garvey also reasoned that the union would be more of a partner with league management through such a deal. For the owners to agree to parting with 55 percent would mean giving about $1.6 billion over four years to the players. Each of the 28 team bosses scoffed at the idea. But Garvey had sold the players on it, claiming they were getting south of 30 percent of those revenues.

"In 1982, there were some bitter feelings on both sides," New York Giants defensive end Gary Jeter told the *Los Angeles Times*. "We hadn't seen the owners' books and when we finally were able to see them, we were upset at the percentage [of revenues] we were receiving. It wasn't fair."

The NFL saw strikes in 1982 and 1987.

On Pro Football Before

"Guys were willing to sit out the whole season. We weren't making any money. We were called professional ballplayers, but we weren't being paid like professional ballplayers. There was no severance. We didn't have as good a pension. Overall benefits weren't as good." —*New York Giants defensive end Gary Jeter*

AUDIBLE

Garvey's counterpart for the NFL's Management Council was Jack Donlan, appointed by the owners to negotiate for them—and perhaps break the union, something Donlan had a reputation for. After negotiating new TV contracts in the spring that doubled rights fees from the networks to $2 billion, Commissioner Pete Rozelle left the labor bargaining to Donlan and a select few powerful owners.

On September 20, the union called for a strike. The owners, instead of looking for replacement players as they would do during the 1987 impasse, locked out the players.

No players crossed picket lines—where could they go with the teams shutting down facilities? The NFLPA staged two exhibition games that flopped. The networks found alternate programming, which generally also flopped. Each side sued in court and got nowhere.

Then the players got nervous, not liking the idea of no earnings—and no shot at a championship—for the rest of the calendar year. Not that the owners liked that scenario, either, but they were more entrenched, more solidified. And, frankly, richer.

The union backed off some demands in November. Pressured by his constituents, Garvey reached an agreement on November 16 to a deal not much different than what the owners had offered during the summer.

The players did gain several important benefits not tied to their earnings. A structured salary system began to develop; no longer would starters find themselves earning less than their backups. But the owners, who lost millions in revenues with seven weeks gone from the season, didn't lose control of revenue splits.

Players had lost an average of $6,000 a week in wages during the strike, and the owners returned $50 million to their broadcast partners.

While ratifying the agreement, the San Francisco 49ers players asked Garvey to resign. He'd lost his power base and resigned the next June.

But the labor game had been changed as both sides hardened. In future years, the players, desperately wanting free agency and more guaranteed money in their contracts, struck again in 1987. This time the owners went with replacement games. Lots of big-name players, including Joe Montana and Lawrence Taylor, eventually crossed picket lines.

At the other end, the owners steadfastly avoided any effective form of player movement. That freedom did come in '93, but the owners got a salary cap to accompany it beginning in 1994.

A period of cooperation followed, particularly when former Raiders star guard Gene Upshaw was running the union and Paul Tagliabue, Rozelle's successor, was commissioner. Player salaries spiked, although the fully guaranteed contracts that baseball and basketball had remained elusive in the NFL.

But Upshaw died in 2008, and a new regime led by powerhouse lawyer DeMaurice Smith was chosen by the players to take them into the next collective bargaining agreement talks in 2011. Smith's agenda was clear: The NFLPA must have a bigger share of the pie, a stronger partnership with the owners. Emboldened by the strength of the baseball and basketball unions, football players showed no fear of a potential lockout. They reasoned that NFL owners, now a billionaire's club, were earning more than enough to give the workers a bigger share. A fairer share.

Unable to agree on a new CBA, the owners locked out the union in March.

The owners, however, had equal resolve—as long as the labor stoppage didn't affect the regular season, and potentially cost them nine figures in lost earnings.

Unable to agree on a new CBA, the owners locked out the union in March. As soon as the prospect of needing to cancel preseason games, then regular-season contests, loomed in midsummer, though, an unprecedented 10-year agreement was struck.

Maybe both sides had learned from the ugliness of 1982 and 1987. At least until 2021, pro football has labor peace.

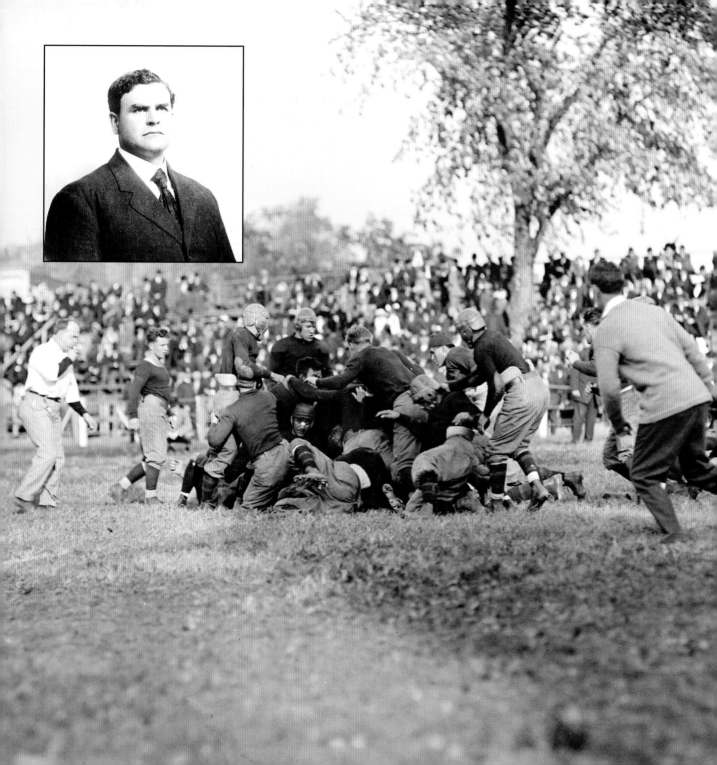

Pop Warner

Growing Grass Roots Football

Glenn Scobey "Pop" Warner was a cunning rascal, the leading lion of the football jungle at the turn of the 20th century. He was crafty and imaginative and became famous while coaching the Carlisle Indians and an amazing Indian athlete named Jim Thorpe.

NO. 30

Warner's active mind explored every facet of coaching football. He was the first to teach the spiral punt and one of the first to advocate the spiral pass; one of the first to introduce the huddle and the double-wing formation, with an unbalanced line for more blocking strength.

Warner coached at six schools but is mostly identified with Carlisle Indian Industrial School. His time there covered 13 seasons (1899–1903, 1907–1914), during which Warner and Thorpe came together in one of the most successful coach-player relationships in football history. "It was the easiest coaching assignment I ever had," said Warner of the powerful teams at Carlisle.

Along the way, Warner managed to bend regulations a bit, keeping a step ahead of football's rules committee. During the 1908 season, in a second stint with Carlisle, Warner came up with a beauty of a trick play.

The rules allowed players to wear elbow pads, so Warner outfitted his team with a special set of pads that looked like a football when a player's arms were crossed at the chest.

Defenders were baffled. It was hard for them to figure out which Carlisle player was carrying the ball.

Before a Harvard-Carlisle game, Harvard coach Percy Haughter was furious. "Pop, the rules permit elbow pads, but the rules also state that the home team can choose the ball," Haughter said to Warner. "Unless you remove those pads, I'll paint the ball red, white and blue."

Warner removed the pads.

Pop Warner and his Carlisle team in 1912

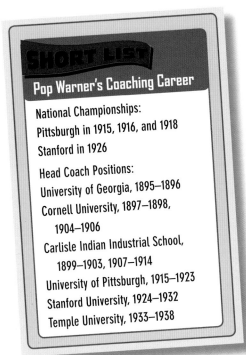

SHORT LIST

Pop Warner's Coaching Career

National Championships:
Pittsburgh in 1915, 1916, and 1918
Stanford in 1926

Head Coach Positions:
University of Georgia, 1895–1896
Cornell University, 1897–1898,
   1904–1906
Carlisle Indian Industrial School,
   1899–1903, 1907–1914
University of Pittsburgh, 1915–1923
Stanford University, 1924–1932
Temple University, 1933–1938

Warner loved to play tricks, and his Indians just loved to play football. He was always coming up with new ideas to flaunt the rulebook loopholes.

During a practice session the Indians playfully hid the ball under a runner's shirt. Warner decided to use the tactic against Harvard.

Carlisle quarterback Frank Mount Pleasant took the ball from center and jammed it under the back of Charlie Dillon's jersey. All the Harvard players started chasing Mount Pleasant, while Dillon ambled unconcerned to a Carlisle touchdown. The next year, the rules committee outlawed the "Hidden Ball Trick."

Warner coached in a number of memorable games at Carlisle, including the legendary 1912 contest with Army. Carlisle subdued the Cadets 27–6 with Thorpe leading the way as usual. One runback of a punt by Thorpe was among the game's highlights, as told by the *New York Times*:

"The ball went directly to Thorpe on West Point's 45-yard line. It was a high kick, and the Cadets were already gathering around the big Indian when he clutched the falling pigskin in his arms.

"His catch and his start were but one motion. In and out, zigzagging first to one side, then another, while a flying Cadet went hurling through space. Thorpe wormed his way through the entire Army team. Every Cadet in the game had a chance, and every one of them failed. . . . it was a dodging game in which Thorpe matched himself against an entire team and proved the master."

While the beloved Thorpe was spreading his brilliance over the field, one particular Army halfback suffered a broken knee to end his football career. Dwight Eisenhower went on to bigger and better things, as a general and then as president of the United States.

Warner also coached at Georgia, Cornell, Pitt, Stanford, and Temple and compiled a record of 319-166-32. Warner coached teams to four National Championships.

So when Warner, about to start coaching at Temple in 1933, was asked to speak to a newly formed group of young football players, he enthusiastically said, "yes," although his most famous speech to them came in the following spring.

The group had been put together in 1929 when juvenile delinquency seemed to be rampant in Philadelphia. Enter Joseph J. Tomlin. The owner of a factory whose windows were constantly being broken appealed to Tomlin for ideas. Tomlin, the son of immigrant parents, had been an all-city tackle at Frankford High School. He pursued a career on Wall Street, but the Great Depression forced him to return to Philadelphia, and he began his involvement in youth football. Tomlin suggested the factory owners fund an athletic program, and football was chosen. By 1933 they had 16 teams.

On the evening of April 19, 1934, when Warner had been invited to speak, a torrential storm hit Philadelphia. The weather featured high winds, unseasonable cold, and rain mixed with sleet. Other coaches had been invited, but Warner was the only one to show. An excited group of 800 young football players asked loads of questions and at the end of the session, the group decided to call itself the Pop Warner Conference.

The famous Pop Warner name attracted youth players to the conference. By 1938 there were 157 teams. After World War II, teams consisted of 15-year-olds and younger.

Interest in football was increasing across the country and Pop Warner Little Scholars was incorporated as a national nonprofit organization in 1959. The basic concept: The classroom is as important as the playing field.

Players are required to meet academic standards. No tryouts. Every child plays. No individual stats—only team stats. The regional champs compete in the National Championship/Super Bowl at Walt Disney World in December.

The basic concept: The classroom is as important as the playing field.

Pop Warner football has also had to deal with concerns of player safety and the question of concussions in players so young. To combat this, new regulations for Pop Warner were instituted. "All of our head coaches and assistant coaches have to take the training for 'Heads Up Football' from USA Football," said Josh Pruce, director of media relations. "One of the rules is, 'When in Doubt, Sit Out,' and we changed our contact rules, limiting the amount of contact to one-third of the practice time," said Pruce.

Currently, Pop Warner has leagues across 36 states with more than 225,000 youth between the ages of 5 and 16 participating in football, cheer, and dance.

Bill Walsh and the West Coast Offense

The Game Gets Really Offensive

Here's the most amazing fact about Bill Walsh, the man who brought the West Coast Offense to full fruition in the NFL and was nicknamed "The Genius" for it: It took Walsh more than a decade to land a head coaching job in the league.

That's right, the mastermind of the offense that dominated pro football for decades and still is popular and successful couldn't get a team owner to hire him.

Walsh learned from some of the great football minds: Marv Levy, Paul Brown, and Sid Gillman. In Walsh's eight seasons with the Bengals, the franchise Brown created, that team's offense flourished. But Walsh didn't get along with Brown and was passed over for the head coaching position when Brown retired after the 1975 season.

Then Walsh spent one year with San Diego, the team Gillman and Don Coryell had taken to prominence through prolific air attacks.

But Walsh had to go to Stanford for two years—the Cardinal went 17-7 in that span—before the San Francisco 49ers came calling.

It became the perfect marriage.

"The essence of Bill Walsh was that he was an extraordinary teacher," NFL commissioner Roger Goodell said. "If you gave him a blackboard and a piece of chalk, he would become a whirlwind of wisdom. He taught all of us not only about football but also about life and how it takes teamwork for any of us to succeed as individuals."

San Francisco 49ers quarterback Joe Montana leading his West Coast Offense

On Coaching for Playmakers

"The thing he did is he really went about putting the game in players' hands, and saying 'you've got to make plays. I may throw you a five-yard slant, but I expect you to turn it into a 30–40 yard play,' and he knew how to get the ball in his players' hands." —*Super Bowl–winning NFL coach and offensive guru Gary Kubiak*

AUDIBLE

Added Hall of Fame cornerback Willie Brown after Walsh died in 2007: "He and [Al] Davis and Sid Gillman were way ahead of their time when it comes to the passing game. You knew he definitely was well ahead of everyone else."

The 49ers were behind the entire NFL when Walsh joined them in 1979. San Francisco drafted a Notre Dame quarterback who supposedly didn't have the arm for the pros, Joe Montana, in the third round. Montana was one of many wise draft picks that would provide the foundation of a dynasty.

Then Walsh set about installing his brand of offense, which soon would be the rage of the league. And what were the identifying qualities of the West Coast Offense? First, the right kind of players:

- A quarterback who was mobile, accurate, and courageous (sound like Montana?).
- Receivers who ran precise routes so the quarterback could depend on them being where he was throwing, and then could break short passes into long gainers.
- Running backs like Roger Craig who could run crisp routes, had good hands, but also could block. A power-running fullback who could catch the ball also fit nicely.
- Tight ends who could get downfield, especially over the middle and in the seams of zone coverages. They had to be strong blockers, too, but were pass catchers first.
- Offensive linemen with mobility to protect in a moving pocket and who were adept at zone blocking.

Walsh's first attempt at the West Coast Offense came with the Bengals after his prize rookie QB, Greg Cook, tore his rotator cuff in the third week of the schedule. So Walsh basically junked what had been a deep passing attack similar to Gillman's and went with the short game based on timing and emphasizing ball control. No more deep drops by the quarterback; three steps or five steps would do. Lots of in-cuts, flare passes, and slants—soon to become as dangerous as any play when Jerry Rice was catching them. Plenty of motion in the backfield.

Much of the West Coast Offense operated inside 15 yards from scrimmage. The idea was to spread the defenders across the field as they tried to thwart the short routes. That opened up the longer passes.

It also aided the run game, which in a reversal of previous philosophies for most teams, was set up by the pass under Walsh.

Critical to it all was how the Niners practiced.

Much of the West Coast Offense operated inside 15 yards from scrimmage.

"Bill always used to say this: 'If you don't put the time in during the week, you don't have a chance on that given Sunday or Monday night,'" Rice recalled to ESPN. "That's why we practiced the way we played during the week. If you came to a 49ers practice, you would not believe the speed of play, the tempo, the attention to detail."

With Walsh at the helm and Montana running the offense so brilliantly, the 49ers won Super Bowls after the 1981, '84, and '88 seasons. In each of those seasons, they scored at least 357 points.

Walsh stepped down as coach—something he later regretted—after the Niners edged Cincinnati, his former team, for the third title. With hand-picked George Seifert, a defensive coach of all things, in charge, the 49ers won again the next year, posting history's most lop-sided Super Bowl victory, 55–10 over Denver.

One of Walsh's least-recognized traits was his understanding of how to build a strong defense. Seifert oversaw a unit that included such draft choices as Ronnie Lott, Keena Turner, Jim Stuckey, Eric Wright, Carlton Williamson, Riki Ellison, Michael Carter, Don Griffin, and Charles Haley. Lott and Haley are Hall of Famers.

"He was a perfectionist," said Turner, a linebacker with the Niners for 11 years before becoming a coach. "When writing his script, he didn't believe that running the football was the way to get there. It had to be prettier than that—beautiful in some way."

Anyone associated with the 49ers in their heyday certainly found the Walsh way beautiful. So did some of his main competitors, who admired more than the football aspect of Walsh.

"Very few of us will leave legacies like he left in this game," current Rams coach Jeff Fisher said. "He brought professionalism to the sport from ownership all the way down to the security people at the front door of the building. He taught people to treat people with respect. What he wanted people to know is that everybody meant something."

No-Huddle and Spread Offenses

The Game Gets Even *More* Offensive

Hurry up!

If it seems that college and pro offenses can't run plays often or fast enough these days, well, you are not watching a video game. It's the real thing.

Nowhere is that more evident than in college football. With the advent of the spread attacks championed by such coaches as Mike Leach and Art Briles—even the Big Ten and SEC, bastions of power ball, have adapted—the Saturday games (and those midweek night affairs) often take on a Wild West flavor. You know, shoot-outs.

And guess what: It's a phenomenon built from the high school level.

"It started with my first football job, coaching in Hamlin (Texas) in '84-85," Baylor coach Briles told SB Nation. "My first year there, we had a great football team, ran the split-back veer, went 13-0-1. In the second year, I saw that if you got deep in the playoffs, you're going to face people with talent just as good or better than yours. So what I looked for was an edge, something different; so in '85 we went to the one-back, four wides and went 14-1.

"When we got to Stephenville (a school that hadn't made the state playoffs in 36 years), we definitely had to do something that gave ourselves a chance to get the opportunity to win football games. We weren't just going to line up and beat people. We had to be a little unconventional, which we were. In 1990 we had a guy throw for over 3,000 yards, and then had a 3,000-yard passer every year over the next 10 years. In '98 we actually set a national record for total offense."

The Patriots brought a lightning-fast, no-huddle offense to Super Bowl XLVI.

Prolific passing attacks hardly are new to football on any level. Some of the greatest Hall of Famers built their careers on the deep ball, whether it was Joe Namath or Dan Fouts chucking it, Lance Alworth or Don Maynard hauling it in.

But since the turn of the century, quick-paced offenses have become the norm. No longer is having a monster defense enough to win championships. There might be the occasional outlier, such as the 2015 Broncos or 2013 Seahawks, but remember, Seattle scored 43 points in the Super Bowl.

As for the colleges, well, consider these recent championship game scores: Ohio State 42, Oregon 20; Florida State 34, Auburn 31; Alabama 42, Notre Dame 14; Alabama 37, Texas 21; LSU 38, Ohio State 24; Florida 41, Ohio State 14; Texas 41, Southern California 38; Southern California 55, Oklahoma 19.

Also consider these stats, which stem not from sloppy offensive performances filled with turnovers, or from special teams running wild. They emanate from the popularity of the spreads, of the no-huddles, and the increasing rules favoring the guys with the ball.

In 1999, NCAA Division I scoring averaged 25.6 points per team and offenses gained 365.3 yards per game. Ten years later, when Briles and his followers were speeding up everything, the numbers were 27.0 and 377.5. And just four years after that, teams were scoring at a 29.4 clip and gaining 411.3 yards.

Why? The passing game.

In '99, college ball still focused on the run in most conferences; teams averaged 212.5 yards passing. By 2012, that stat soared to 238.3.

Quarterbacks are being groomed from junior high school. They begin attending passing camps when they barely are in their teens. By the time they get to high school, they are primed for throwing the ball all over the field because they've had hundreds of repetitions in seven-on-seven drills.

NFL data are just as enlightening:

Pass plays increased from 69.6 per game in 1998 to 75.9 in 2013.

Quarterbacks have never been more protected by the rules. Receivers have never been less encumbered in their routes.

In 1998, the 32 teams scored 20.8 points an outing. In 2013, that average reached a record 23.4.

And don't forget all the rules changes that benefit the offense. When fans hear defenders complaining how unfair things are, well, they don't really care that those defensive players have a genuine beef.

Quarterbacks have never been protected more by the rules, which enables them to send more receivers into patterns and allows them to feel braver in the pocket. Receivers have never been less encumbered in their routes. So, again, coaches get as many guys as possible downfield.

"They don't let the defenses do their thing anymore," former Ravens standout linebacker Ray Lewis said. "The NFL wants points, they want TV ratings, they don't think defense sells."

Offensive coordinators can't always outfox their defensive counterparts, but they can force mismatches by not huddling, or going up-tempo. They also can wear out a defense that doesn't get the opportunity to substitute.

"The defense needs to prepare differently for a no-huddle offense," longtime offensive coordinator and head coach Chan Gailey told SB Nation. "They must shift into second gear. If we can cause them to spend 10 minutes of practice time a day on developing a different form of communication, that translates into 40 minutes of preparation time spent on something other than defending the actual plays. . . . Also, defense elicits a great deal of emotion—slapping each other, pumping up each other, etc. This is almost eliminated since there is no time to regroup."

SHORT LIST

The Top Five Highest Scoring Teams in NFL History

Denver in 2013 (606)

New England in 2007 (589)

Green Bay in 2011 (560)

New England in 2012 (557)

Minnesota in 1998 (556)

The no-huddle should not be misinterpreted. It does not mean always calling plays at breakneck speed, running the two-minute drill for 60 minutes or passing on every down. The idea, in great part, is to make the defense think you will be hurrying up, preventing substitutions (unless the offense brings in replacements) and, perhaps, preventing the D from doing what it does best.

Of course, it is pushing things if a team doesn't have a quarterback capable of playing comfortably at a heightened pace. Tom Moore, the mastermind when Peyton Manning was burning up the league in Indianapolis, perfectly explains the reasoning for the no-huddle, the hurry-up, and the spread.

"When the going gets tough and you don't have a lot of time left and you have to score to win the game, you have to use the two-minute offense," Moore said. "Well, the more I got to thinking about it, why shouldn't it be good the first two minutes of the game?"

And now just about everyone feels that way.

Vince Lombardi

The Man Who (May Have) Said, "Winning isn't everything. It's the only thing."

In 1959, the once-proud Green Bay Packers were the joke of the NFL. The year before, the Packers had only won a single game.

The Packers sent out a call for help to Vince Lombardi, who was having success as the offensive coordinator of the New York Giants. It was a call that Lombardi had been waiting for all his life.

While helping to build the Giants into an NFL power, Lombardi was hoping to land a job as a head coach somewhere in the NFL. Lombardi not only landed the head coaching job in Green Bay, he also talked Packers management into giving him the position as general manager.

NO. **33**

It was a bold move by Lombardi, who still had to prove himself as the absolute leader of a team. Starting out with a troubled squad like Green Bay after the Packers went 1-10-1 in 1958, he knew finding success would be tough.

As the widely syndicated sportswriter Red Smith said: the pre-Lombardi 1-10-1 Packers "overwhelmed one opponent, underwhelmed 10 and whelmed one" in 1958.

Lombardi turned the Packers around virtually overnight.

The Packers lost the NFL title game in 1960, but not much more after that. In the next seven years, the Packers won five championships, including the famous "Ice Bowl" game in 1967 against the Dallas Cowboys played in Green Bay's brutally cold conditions.

Temperatures were clocked at 13 below zero at game time, turning the Packers' field into an ice rink. Frank Gifford opened the TV broadcast saying, "I just took a bite out of my coffee." When the referee blew the first play dead and removed the whistle, part of his

They named the Super Bowl trophy after the legendary Green Bay coach.

lip came with it. It bled briefly, and then froze. After that, there were no whistles in the Ice Bowl. They used voice and hand commands to officiate the rest of the game.

Green Bay had an early 14–0 lead, but in the fourth quarter, with 4:50 left, it was behind 17–14. So Green Bay quarterback Bart Starr moved the Packers down the field, cool as the 18 degrees below zero weather. The Packers were two feet from a touchdown when Starr called a timeout with 16 seconds remaining. It was the Packers' last timeout.

Starr approached Lombardi on the sideline and they conferred. It was decided that Starr would keep the ball on a quarterback sneak, following Jerry Kramer into the end zone. "Run it," Lombardi said, "and let's get the hell out of here!"

So Starr surprised everyone, diving over for the score and a 21–17 Packers victory for the league championship. Soon after, the Pack would win their second straight Super Bowl.

What made Lombardi so great that his name now graces the Super Bowl trophy?

He was ruthless in his approach to football, pushing his teams harder than you can imagine. In practice, Lombardi the perfectionist made his players repeat plays until they were spotless. As one player said, "He pushed you and pushed you and made you strong."

Lombardi's coaching career was filled with oft-repeated quotable sayings. The most repeated: "Winning isn't everything—it's the only thing."

But Lombardi said the quote wasn't quite right. The actual quote, he said: "Winning isn't everything, but wanting to win is."

He did his share of winning, starting with his college career at Fordham in New York City, where he played right guard on the legendary Seven Blocks of Granite line. The team was coached by Jim Crowley, one of the memorable Four Horsemen of Notre Dame in the 1920s.

On Football as an American Symbol

"I've been in football all my life, gentlemen, and I don't know whether I'm particularly qualified to be part of anything else, except I consider it a great game, a game of many assets, by the way, and I think a symbol of what this country's best attributes are: courage and stamina and a coordinated efficiency or teamwork." —*Vince Lombardi*

AUDIBLE

Lombardi's toughness could not be exaggerated. In a game against Pitt in his senior year (1936), Lombardi suffered a deep gash inside his mouth. He was taken out of the game and remained on the sideline until Crowley brought him back to anchor a goal-line stand against the Panthers. The stand preserved a scoreless tie for the Rams, who later lost a 7–6 decision to NYU for their first defeat of the season.

Of course, he did his share of winning as a coach, starting at St. Cecilia High School in Englewood, New Jersey, where he developed a powerhouse, at one point winning 36 straight games. Actually, Lombardi started his coaching career in basketball at St. Cecilia. In 1943, Lombardi's football team was recognized as the top high school squad in the country.

When he arrived in Green Bay in 1959, he was 46 years old and desperate to prove himself as a head coach.

Lombardi, who had at one time thought about a career in law, continued along the coaching path with jobs at Fordham and the U.S. Military Academy. Then he joined the Giants and worked with Tom Landry, another future Hall of Fame coach, before the Packers came calling.

So when he arrived in Green Bay in 1959, he was 46 years old and desperate to prove himself as a head coach. The first thing he did was issue an ultimatum: Lombardi's decisions were never to be questioned. He ran the football team on and off the field. With the power to do so, he traded freely.

"My first problem was one of organization," Lombardi said. "On and off the field. Then I wanted to strengthen our defense, and I worked hard at it."

He traded for experienced and tough players. He felt there was no substitute for defensive experience. "Our offense wasn't that good," said Lombardi, "so I concentrated on defense."

At the beginning. Later, the Packers' star offensive power exploded with players such as Paul Hornung, Jim Taylor, Starr, and Kramer. Lombardi moved Hornung from fullback to halfback and the great running back responded as a tremendous ground and receiving threat.

In his nine seasons at Green Bay from 1959 to 1967, Lombardi led one of the NFL's true dynasty teams. Lombardi's teams went 141-39-4 and boasted a winning percentage of .783. As the Packers continued to win, their popularity soared.

"We were the first dynasty of the TV era," Hornung said. "First, we got a lot more publicity in the Midwest when we beat the Bears. Then, when we beat the Giants, Madison Avenue awakened to us."

Lovers of the underdog wanted to see the smallest town in the league beating up the biggest city in the country.

They did, thanks to Lombardi.

Gene Upshaw, Ed Garvey, and the NFLPA

Fighting for Freedom of Movement

It's difficult to fathom in these days of $20-million-a-year quarterbacks and salary caps approaching $200 million that there was a time of no free agency, no agents representing players, no union.

If a pro football player didn't like what he was getting paid, he generally couldn't shop his wares elsewhere—except for the occasional times when another league cropped up such as the AAFC, the AFL, or the USFL.

In 1956, while the AAFC was sending three franchises to the NFL, efforts to form a players' association began. Several players approached Creighton Miller, former general manager for the Cleveland Browns and an attorney, about starting a union. Miller sought the support of some of the NFL's biggest names, from Norm Van Brocklin of the Rams to Frank Gifford of the Giants, and other team leaders such as Don Shula of the Colts. Early into the 1956 season a majority of the league's players signed authorizations to allow Miller and the new NFLPA to represent them. Only one team at the time, the Bears, had not joined in.

The players requested of team owners a minimum $5,000 salary; set per diem pay; a rule requiring clubs to pay for equipment; and, as the primary item on the players' agenda, continued payment of a player's salary if he was injured.

"We made arrangements with the commissioner [Bert Bell] to go to Philadelphia during the owners' meeting," Miller said. "Bert put us up at the Racquet Club and the owners were meeting at some hotel. We got there maybe on a Sunday night and Kyle Rote had to leave

DeMaurice F. "De" Smith was elected Executive Director of the NFLPA on March 15, 2009. Note the Gene Upshaw pin.

SHORT LIST

Average Player Salaries

Year	Average player salary	Median salary
1980	$79,000	$50,000
1985	$217,000	$160,000
1990	$354,000	$275,000
1995	$584,000	$301,000
2000	$787,000	$441,000
2005	$1.4M	$569,000
2007	$1.75M	$772,000
2013	$1.9M	$770,000
2015	$2.1M	$860,000

on Wednesday and Norm Van Brocklin left about Friday. I was still there Saturday, and we never did get a chance to meet with the owners and we never got a response."

By ignoring the requests, the owners reinforced the players' resolve. They threatened to sue each team and the NFL itself, which believed that like Major League Baseball it owned antitrust exemptions. It did not, and when one antitrust case went against the owners in the Supreme Court, they changed course and granted many of the players' demands.

The NFL Players Association grew through the 1960s' AFL/NFL talent wars, eventually merging into a certified union in 1970.

Then began in earnest the struggles over such issues as minimum salaries, pension, insurance, health benefits, and freedom of movement. With attorney Ed Garvey hired in 1971 as the NFLPA's first executive director, the players filed a lawsuit to overturn the Rozelle Rule, which effectively stopped players from moving to another team once their contracts expired. That would become the union's lengthiest battle with the NFL.

In 1974, with free agency the major issue, the players staged a summer strike. But it collapsed because team owners didn't respond to any of the demands, and the union called off the walkout, again going to the courts and the NLRB with their cases.

By the next year, more than half the NFL players no longer were paying union dues, which led to a 1977 collective bargaining agreement that heavily favored management. Even though the Rozelle Rule ended, the commissioner still held the power to rule on free agency, with hefty compensation to teams losing players. In other words, little to no player movement.

The NFLPA needed to be more forceful, even if that meant taking money out of players' pockets in the short run—for better salary and benefits over the long haul.

A 1982 strike saw the players propose a revenue split in which they would get 55 percent of the clubs' league-wide income. Basically, the owners chuckled and the first NFL season disrupted by a labor stoppage hit (see Game Changer 29). Seven games per team were canceled that season, and nothing concrete in the way of player movement was achieved. The union did secure an enhanced salary and benefit package, and approval of agent certification to represent players in negotiations.

The next battle came in 1987, and again the union resorted to a strike—the last the league has witnessed—under new leadership of Hall of Fame guard Gene Upshaw. One of his first moves after replacing Garvey was to poll the players on their priorities. Legitimate free agency was top.

In 2011, owners locked out the players from March through most of July before a 10-year agreement was reached.

"Our players view freedom of movement as essential to a fair CBA," Upshaw said before the strike, during which the teams used replacement players and 15 percent of union members crossed picket lines.

Having flopped again with its work stoppage, it had become clear to the NFLPA that fighting the NFL in court was the most effective way to reach some of its goals. And they began having success.

It also helped that Upshaw and Paul Tagliabue, who became NFL commissioner in 1989, developed a strong working relationship. Both understood that as the revenue pie grew, all sides could prosper through labor peace.

In 1989, fearing the courts would implement total free agency, the league instituted Plan B, which allowed franchises to protect 37 players, while the rest had two months to sign elsewhere without compensation. Late that year, the players voted to decertify the union.

Of course, that was not the end of the NFLPA. Rather, it was re-formed as a professional association dedicated to protecting the individual contracting rights of players. And that's when the NLRB and the courts began finding in favor of the players.

Plan B was shot down by a jury in September 1992 in Freeman McNeil's suit against the league. That was a landmark decision. Other NFLPA wins followed. The next year, Tagliabue and Upshaw struck the first CBA that included true free agency. The owners got a salary cap in return, and the players received a percentage of revenues; 58 percent was the number in 1993.

The NFLPA was cleared to become a union once more. For the next 15 years, until Upshaw passed away in 2008, work stoppages were avoided. Critics claimed Upshaw settled for less than he could have gotten from the league, which in 2006 replaced the retiring Tagliabue with Roger Goodell. They said Upshaw's relationship with management was too cozy.

Current executive director DeMaurice Smith and his constituency have an uneasy, often contentious alliance with the league. In 2011, owners locked out the players from March through most of July before a 10-year agreement was reached. Ever since, the two sides have been at odds on many issues, including drug testing, player safety, length of the season, and the NFL's personal conduct policy.

Joe Paterno's Grand Experiment

Campaigning to Increase Academic Standards for College Athletes

NO. **35**

Academics and athletics—Joe Paterno was about to start the "Grand Experiment."

Would it work? The Penn State football coach was about to find out in the 1965 season as he launched the student-athlete era at Penn State, with the emphasis on student.

Students first, athletics second. And why not add life skills?

- Take care of the little things and the big things will take care of themselves.

- Keep plugging away and something good will happen.

- Respect your peers and your elders.

- Don't cut corners.

Once Matt Joyner, who played at Penn State from 1995 to 1998, was about to grab lunch between practices. "I figured I'll just cut across the grass." Paterno screamed at Matt to get off the grass. To Paterno it was symbolic of taking shortcuts in life.

Today Paterno and Penn State are synonymous. It wasn't always so. When Paterno, a star quarterback at Brown University and a disciple of Rip Engle, came to Penn State in 1950, he didn't expect to stay. He was there to earn tuition for law school. His father had earned his law degree at age 40 by going to school at night, and expected big things from his son.

Joe Paterno's teams produced 47 academic All-Americans.

On Students First, Athletes Second

"We're just kidding ourselves if we think we can bring kids in with minimal credentials and have them play football or basketball and get a meaningful education." —*Joe Paterno*

AUDIBLE

But Paterno loved coaching and decided to make it his life's work. His parents were not as enthusiastic. Angelo Paterno finally offered his blessing with one caveat: "Make an impact."

After 16 years as Engle's assistant, Joe Paterno became head coach. In the beginning, it was tough. The 38-year-old lost three of his first five games. When the Nittany Lions finished 5-5 in 1966 and opened the 1967 season with a loss to Navy, Paterno wasn't so sure he belonged in football. "I was wondering whether I really had it," Paterno recalled.

After a loss to UCLA, Penn State quickly turned things around—31 straight games without a defeat.

During this time, Paterno went public with his "Grand Experiment." He continued to campaign for education throughout his coaching career, helping lead a national campaign to increase academic standards for college athletes.

Dave Joyner, Matt's father, played on the offensive line for some of Paterno's best teams from 1969 to 1971. He was one of thousands who benefited from Paterno's wise counsel. Joyner's time at Penn State was a springboard to a medical career.

"At first you have no idea what Paterno is talking about," Matt Joyner said. "Then in your junior year, the light starts to go on. OK, I'm not learning about football, I'm learning about life. That's what Joe is teaching me.

"He's not only teaching me about sports, he's teaching me about how you deal with your family, how you interact with people from a professional standpoint, and how you deal with adversity within your life."

Welcome to the Joe Paterno Finishing School, and a team with one of the highest graduation rates for college football players in the country. Oh, by the way, mix in some solid football—a record 409 victories, and two National Championships.

Part of Paterno's philosophy: "I've always preached to my boys, there's one thing I want you to do, and this is don't ever be afraid to lose. If you're afraid to lose, you don't have a chance of winning."

His philosophy was summed up in the Orange Bowl game of 1969 when Paterno went for a risky two-point conversion instead of the safer extra point kick after a touchdown. The result: a 15–14 Penn State victory.

At the time, Paterno was in the early days of an unmatched career. He was head coach at State College from 1966 to 2011, 46 seasons. Coupled with his 15 years as Engle's assistant, that made Paterno a coaching veteran of 62 years at Penn State before his death in 2012.

In that time, he was equally proud of his players' academic achievements. In 2011, Paterno generated an 87 percent graduation-success rate to tie Stanford for first among ranked teams. Paterno's teams produced 47 academic All-Americans, including 15 from 2006 to 2010.

Paterno, who had donated millions of dollars to the campus library, seemed as if he would last forever at Penn State—indeed, his critics thought he had overstayed his welcome as he headed past his 80th birthday. Then a shocking scandal stunned the campus.

It hit like a bombshell, not only at Penn State but all across the country. A coach on Paterno's staff, Jerry Sandusky, was arrested for child molestation.

Paterno, in the midst of fighting lung cancer, was fired by Penn State's board of directors. Though Paterno had notified Penn State administrators when he learned of the abuse, the trustees felt he hadn't gone far enough. They had the Paterno statue that had stood at Beaver Stadium removed. It wasn't even close to the kind of punishments and sanctions that the NCAA handed him and the school.

It hit like a bombshell, not only at Penn State but all across the country.

In a series of unprecedented moves, Penn State would pay $60 million to the NCAA over five years, Penn State was stripped of four postseason bowl games in the next four years, and the Nittany Lions were stripped of 10 football scholarships per year over the next four years. In addition, the NCAA vacated 112 of Paterno's victories.

Many of the sanctions would be lifted in 2015, including a full complement of scholarships. Paterno's victory total of 409 was restored to put him back as the coach with the most victories in major college football history.

Joe Paterno's legacy will have little to do with a scandal. He made an impact on college football, his players, the Penn State community, and the Grand Experiment he championed.

Bear Bryant
Building Alabama's Roll Tide Dynasty

The legend of Paul "Bear" Bryant was not built on how he got his nickname.

Oh, sure, it's a great tale: According to the *Encyclopedia of Alabama*, a teenage Bryant attended a traveling circus. At a sideshow at the Lyric Theater in Fordyce, Alabama, Bryant accepted the challenge to wrestle a bear. For every minute young Paul lasted, he would earn a dollar.

When the Bear's muzzle came off, Bryant quickly left the ring—he never got paid. He did, however, earn a nickname that lasted a lifetime.

NO. **36**

But Bryant's legacy was built on what he meant to and what he did for college football.

Generally regarded as the greatest coach the game has seen, Bryant was about much more than the numbers, though they are very impressive numbers. See the Short List sidebar!

In part, what made Bryant such an important figure in the sport was his impact on his home state, where, as the joke goes, there are two seasons: spring football and fall football. There are no professional major league teams in Alabama, so Crimson Tide and Auburn Tigers football is akin to religion from Tuscaloosa to Talladega and everywhere in between.

Marc Torrence, a former sports editor of *Crimson White*, the school's official newspaper, explained it to al.com: "Whenever people talk about the great college football coaches, you hear Bear Bryant and Woody Hayes, guys who sort of transcended their generation," Torrence said. "I knew who he was just from that. Whenever you talked about legendary coaches, Bear Bryant's name was always in the picture.

"Once I got here, you could really see just how much of an effect Bear Bryant has on people's lives and this campus, especially for the people who were around when he was here.

Alabama Crimson Tide head coach Paul "Bear" Bryant on the sideline against the Auburn Tigers

SHORT LIST

Bear Bryant by the Numbers

* 323-85-17 record at Maryland, Kentucky, Texas A&M, and Alabama
* 5 Associated Press National Championships * 4 Undefeated Seasons (3 with Alabama and 1 with Texas A&M) * 29 Bowl Games (15-12-2 bowl-game record)

I've never heard somebody talk about a man in such a godlike way. People who are 60 and 70 talk about Bear Bryant in such awe and reverence. You see his influence not just in football. He's just a god around here."

Some credit Bryant with developing elements of the spread offense and inventing the shovel pass. What can't be disputed was his mastery of the Wishbone. Immediately following Alabama's 24–24 tie with Oklahoma in the 1970 Bluebonnet Bowl, Bryant went to work on the newfangled attack that the Sooners had used effectively in the game. The Crimson Tide had gone 6-5 and 6-5-1, and Bryant needed answers.

He recognized the potential and how his players could fit perfectly into the run-oriented offense featuring a fullback behind the quarterback and in front of two tailbacks, forming a wishbone in the backfield.

The formation had been introduced by coach Darrell Royal at Texas, and many schools would run it for years—but none more successfully than Alabama. "It could be said the decision to go to the Wishbone saved coach Bryant's career, or extended it," Royal said. "I'm glad I was able to contribute to that because he was truly an exceptional coach. He took the Wishbone to another level."

Bryant went 11-1 in 1971 with the Wishbone as the base of his offense. His Tide teams won 97 games the rest of the decade, taking the national title in 1978 and 1979.

Bryant had made another major decision at the end of the 1960s, one that would affect college football throughout the South. Seeing how dominant African-American players had become in other areas of the nation, Bryant told the university's administrators that the school needed to move into modern times. There is no evidence that Bryant saw himself as a pioneer in breaking the color barrier in the Southeastern Conference. He simply was being pragmatic.

A game against Southern California (see Game Changer 27), which for years had been led by star black players, fully convinced not only Bryant but his superiors at Alabama that a segregated football team couldn't be a championship team anymore. Nothing much altruistic there.

Running back Wilbur Jackson was in the stands for that game and became the first African American offered a football scholarship by the Crimson Tide. Defensive lineman John Mitchell became the first black starter for Alabama and later coached for Bryant before coaching in the NFL.

"Growing up in Alabama, you either wanted to go to Alabama or Auburn. It didn't matter if you were black, brown, green or yellow," said Mitchell, from Mobile. "I knew Alabama had won a couple of national championships and everybody knew who coach Bryant was. It would have been an honor to walk on."

It was no coincidence that Bryant's team began winning so regularly again once he turned to the Wishbone and opened the doors to black players.

To cast Bryant as a gentle fatherly figure, however, would be a stretch. Nothing illustrated that better than his days with the Junction Boys. In 1954, Bryant took his Texas A&M players some 300 miles from campus for a summer training camp in which he would "separate the quitters from the keepers." It was his first season coaching the Aggies, and Bryant was all about making a statement. Players who attended have described the camp as "10 days in hell" or "the worst experience of my life." More than 100 began the training sessions, which rarely featured water breaks and during which the coaches often ignored injuries. Bryant found lots of quitters: Nearly three-quarters of the Junction Boys didn't make it through, heading home early instead.

Players who attended have described the camp as "10 days in hell" or "the worst experience of my life."

As Gene Stallings, a player then and later a National Championship coach at Alabama, told Jim Dent, the author of the book *The Junction Boys*: "We went out there in two buses and came back in one."

The NCAA outlawed such camps the next year. Thus, Bryant inadvertently had a game-changing role years before he coached the Crimson Tide.

Bryant feared retirement, and 37 days after he left coaching in 1983, the state of Alabama mourned the passing of The Bear.

NFL Free Agency

Football Moves from Plan B to Its Own Moneyball

Those nine-figure contracts that quarterbacks and pass rushers and receivers grab when they reach the summit of professional football seem something of a norm these days.

Joe Flacco bets on himself, plays out the last year of his deal, and wins a Super Bowl. The payoff: $120 million or so as the Baltimore Ravens keep their championship QB away from the open market.Free agency—or the threat of it—has completely changed the financial landscape of pro football, where the average career lasts under four years. It just so happens that, generally, players must have four years or more of service in the NFL to get the chance to strike it rich with a second contract.

Still, freedom has been critical for the players and the owners.

"It has allowed players to share in the windfall of a business that continually grows and will continue to grow," said agent Joe Linta, who masterminded Flacco's deal.

The free agency game can be cutthroat. And success doesn't always depend on the amount of money being offered. Comfort and relationships are key, too.

"It's extremely important because football is a people business, too," Raiders general manager Reggie McKenzie told the *Buffalo News*. "When you get into this age of free agency, you want to keep your good players and try to attract more good players. The way of doing that is the people that you have in your building have to speak highly of you. So they say 'Hey, man, you should come here. It's a good organization.'"

Joe Flacco got a nine-figure deal that kept him off the open market.

AUDIBLE

On the Salary Cap and Team Spending

"The salary cap has kept the free spenders [Dallas, Washington] in check and kept the cheap teams [Bengals, Steelers, Bills] forced to pay out a large portion of their revenues." —*agent Joe Linta*

For decades, in all sports, those organizations owned the rights to their players in perpetuity. Iron-clad contracts didn't allow for any form of freedom.

But free agency already was a topic in baseball as far back as the 1970s. The players' association, which developed into one of the nation's most powerful unions—not just in sports but in the entire labor picture—made it a primary cause, and in 1975 won it in the courts.

It took the NFL much longer. Indeed, the NFLPA was not recognized by the league as the bargaining agent of the players until 1968. That summer, after a brief labor stoppage that was the first in league history, the first collective bargaining agreement between the union and management was reached.

Three years later, when Ed Garvey was hired as NFLPA executive director, the first true volley in football free agency was fired when the union filed an antitrust case against the NFL seeking to eliminate the Rozelle Rule. That rule had called for Commissioner Pete Rozelle awarding equal compensation paid by the team a player joins to a team that saw a player play out his contract and become "free." Except there was no real freedom because the compensation scared off any free-agent pursuers.

Oh, there had been player movement in 1962: Receiver R. C. Owens, he of the "alley-oop" catches, left San Francisco for Baltimore. After that, 49ers owner Vic Morabito would not speak to Colts owner Carroll Rosenbloom. The next year, Rozelle instituted his rule on compensation.

A positive step in the battle for liberation came in 1977, when the union won its antitrust lawsuit in the name of Hall of Fame tight end John Mackey. The only problem was that it led to virtually no more movement of players from team to team unless they were traded.

Indeed, a decade later, when the players struck and the owners hired replacements for three games, free agency still was more of a yearning than a reality for the guys on the field.

At the end of 1987, the NFLPA was back in court, asking federal judge David Doty—who had often ruled in its favor—to negate the league's restrictive free agency system. Although Doty did not overturn the CBA, he believed the players would win their latest antitrust suit. The NFL came up with Plan B free agency. It allowed each franchise to protect 37 players by having the right of first refusal on any offers those players got elsewhere. Because a team could be highly creative in constructing an offer, though, there was the possibility of more movement; remember, there was no salary cap at the time.

Still, it was restrictive because it involved compensation if a player from the protected list of 37 left. Plan B lasted from 1989 to 1992, struck down by a Minneapolis jury that awarded $1.63 million in damages to four of the eight plaintiffs. Two weeks after that, Doty declared Philadelphia's Keith Jackson, Detroit's D. J. Dozier, Cleveland's Webster Slaughter, and New England's Garin Veris unrestricted free agents.

And then, finally, a true free agency system was installed in 1993.

Eagles star defensive end Reggie White filed a class-action suit that the owners sensed he would win. So management sat down with the union, now led by a former player and a Hall of Famer, Gene Upshaw, and hammered out a deal that would include the salary cap to protect teams from the outrageous bidding wars baseball already was going through. The salary cap also would ensure more of a competitive balance because regardless of market and ancillary opportunities, every team had the same number of dollars to spend.

Fittingly, it was pro sports' smallest city, Green Bay, and White himself who struck the free agency deal that would reverberate forever in pro football.

White, 31, left Philadelphia for a four-year, $17 million contract, and the money was significant.

The Packers outbid Washington and San Francisco. That one of the best African-American players in the NFL would opt for northern Wisconsin with its lack of diversity over the nation's capital and the Bay Area was a harbinger.

Pro sports' smallest city, Green Bay, struck the free agency deal that would reverberate forever in pro football.

Further inhibitions on free agency subsequently have been added, particularly the franchise and transition tags clubs can use to keep a key player. In return, though, the player gets a one-year deal for an average salary among the league leaders for his position if he fails to negotiate a long-term agreement. Considering how many millions of dollars that entails, losing that freedom for a while doesn't sound so bad—for either side.

Sammy Baugh and Sid Luckman

These Two Shall Pass

NO. 38

During Sammy Baugh's first practice session with the Washington Redskins, coach Ray Flaherty handed him a football.

"They tell me you're quite a passer," Flaherty said.

"I reckon I can throw a little," said the tall, rangy Texan.

"Show me," Flaherty said. "Hit that receiver in the eye."

To which Baugh supposedly replied, "Which eye?"

Apocryphal or not, the story may be closer to the truth than you think. At the prime of his career in the 1930s and 1940s, Baugh was brimming with confidence and talent, ready to lead the NFL into the modern age with his sharpshooting passing ability.

He would have been considered the greatest quarterback of his era—or any other era, for that matter—except that Sid Luckman also happened to be playing at the same time. Like Baugh, Luckman was a brilliant passer who helped take the NFL to a new place, changing the game of football forever.

Because of their pre-eminent skills, they were constantly compared to each other. It was almost impossible to differentiate between the two in terms of value to their teams—Luckman with the Chicago Bears and Baugh with the Washington Redskins.

Baugh's all-around game was amazing. One season he led the league in passing, interceptions as a defensive back, and punting at a time when players went both ways. Baugh is the only player to lead the NFL in offense, defense, and special teams categories.

"Slingin' Sammy" Baugh in September of 1937

But it was his passing ability that caught everyone's attention in a career with the Redskins from 1937 to 1952.

Baugh grew up in Sweetwater, Texas. He played four years of high school football, but was recruited to play baseball at Texas Christian. "Slingin' Sammy" Baugh earned his nickname as a baseball player. He was a superb all-around athlete who joined the football team and was an All-American as TCU won the 1935 National Championship. At the College All-Star Game he threw the winning touchdown pass to beat the Green Bay Packers, 6–0.

Redskins owner George Preston Marshall picked Baugh in the first round of the NFL's 1936 draft. When Baugh came into the NFL, it was a time when the pass was used only in desperate situations. Baugh (and Luckman) soon changed that.

In that 1937 season, Baugh completed a record 81 passes (about seven a game) and led the league with 1,127 passing yards. Baugh went on to lead the league in passing six seasons in an era when the ground game was still dominant.

In his rookie year, Baugh tossed three touchdown passes to lead the Redskins to a 28–21 victory over the Chicago Bears in the NFL championship game. Baugh led the Redskins to another title in 1942.

Baugh would have liked to forget the NFL championship game in 1940, when the Redskins were slaughtered 73–0 by Luckman's Bears. It still stands as the biggest rout in championship game history. "He did have one of his rare bad days," said Luckman, who completed four of six throws for 102 yards, "but they couldn't do anything right. But he was still the best. With Slingin' Sammy Baugh, you always knew you were in for a hell of a game."

Luckman was a Brooklyn playground legend. "When I was a young boy growing up in Brooklyn, we used to play football for hours on the cobblestone streets," said Luckman. He became a star at Erasmus Hall High School, and then at Columbia University. Columbia did not give athletic scholarships, and Luckman thought he would have to leave school when there was a family financial crisis. His coach, Lou Little, came to the rescue, lining up jobs so he could not only stay in school, but also help his mother. "It was like a dream come true," said Luckman.

George Halas, owner of the Chicago Bears, had invented the T-formation and needed a quarterback to run it.

George Halas, owner of the Chicago Bears, had invented the T-formation and needed a quarterback to run it. He wanted Columbia's All-American for his team.

Luckman turned him down. He didn't think he was big enough to play professional football at 5 feet, 11 inches and 190 pounds. Halas didn't give up. He traveled twice to New York to persuade Luckman to join the Bears.

"When I read in the paper that I had been drafted by the Bears, it was certainly a tremendous surprise," said Luckman. "But I had a very nice job and that's where I thought my future was going to be."

Halas offered Luckman a $5,000 contract. Luckman accepted Halas's offer, but he knew he was in for a rough time when he saw his teammates, nicknamed the "Monsters of the Midway," in the locker room.

"All my high school and college career, I had never seen anything like these athletes," said Luckman of the Bears' line. So he practiced and studied long after the Bears' practices were over.

Although Luckman played his first few games with the Bears as a halfback, he was soon to get his chance as a quarterback. The Bears were in New York playing the Giants and fell behind 16–0.

In the third period, Halas told Luckman to take over as the quarterback.

"You'll never know the emotion, stress," said Luckman of that 1939 game. "My family, friends from college, the Columbia coaches. . . . they were all at the game.

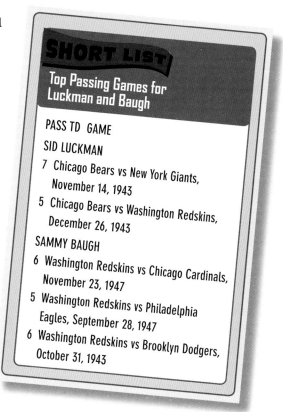

SHORT LIST

Top Passing Games for Luckman and Baugh

PASS TD GAME

SID LUCKMAN

7 Chicago Bears vs New York Giants, November 14, 1943

5 Chicago Bears vs Washington Redskins, December 26, 1943

SAMMY BAUGH

6 Washington Redskins vs Chicago Cardinals, November 23, 1947

5 Washington Redskins vs Philadelphia Eagles, September 28, 1947

6 Washington Redskins vs Brooklyn Dodgers, October 31, 1943

"The football in those days was fatter and bigger, rounder and harder to grip. I threw the greatest pass of my life—wobbly, end to end."

That pass went for a touchdown. The Bears lost the game 16–14, but Luckman was the starting quarterback from then on. The next year he led the team to that 73–0 romp over Baugh and the Redskins.

Over his career he led the Bears to four NFL championships, was voted Most Valuable Player in the NFL three times, and All-Pro seven times. Like Baugh, his pro-passing-game co-pioneer, he is in the Pro Football Hall of Fame.

Platooning

Offensive, Defensive, and Special Teams Units

Platoon: A group of players within a team, especially a football team, that is trained and sent into or withdrawn from play as a unit—the defensive platoon, the offensive platoon, etc.

NO. **39**

Ask anyone in the Philadelphia Eagles' organization who was the best linebacker in the team's history. Chuck Bednarik is usually the name that comes up first.

Ask the same for the center position. The answer? Chuck Bednarik.

Bednarik happened to be superb at two positions and has the distinction as the last of the full-time two-way players in the National Football League—center on offense, linebacker on defense.

It was the era of "Iron Man" football, also known as the one-platoon system, a time when the same players played offense, then defense, then offense again.

They called Bednarik "Concrete Charlie" because he worked for a concrete manufacturer when he wasn't tossing players around on the gridiron like rag dolls. But "concrete" could have very well applied to his hard-nosed play on the field.

Bednarik epitomized the tough-guy linebacker. Also the tough-guy center.

A star at Penn before joining the Eagles in 1949, Bednarik was known for his ferocious hits in 14 years in the NFL. The New York Giants' Frank Gifford was on the receiving end of one of Bednarik's biggest blows in 1960. That hit cost Gifford the rest of that season, all of 1961, and left an indelible mark on the Giants great.

A month after he laid out Gifford, Bednarik made an NFL title game tackle of Green Bay Packers fullback Jim Taylor to save the contest for the Eagles. It clinched a second championship for Bednarik.

A caravan of Cowboys coming off the field

AUDIBLE

On Football That Makes a Man a Lesser Player

"Blocking doesn't teach you to tackle, so what two-platoon football does is make a man a lesser player." —*former Missouri head coach Dan Devine*

On the offensive side, Bednarik was an outstanding center for each of his 14 pro seasons, a regular on All-Pro squads who earned himself a place in the Hall of Fame. In 2010 when the NFL picked its 100 best players of all time, naturally, Bednarik had to be on the list.

Along with the iconic plays involving Gifford and Taylor, there was Bednarik's memorable performance in the 1954 Pro Bowl: He punted in place of the injured Charlie Trippi, and spent the rest of the game winning the MVP award by recovering three fumbles and running an interception for a touchdown.

In 1999 the *Sporting News* placed Bednarik among its own Top 100 NFL Players.

Prior to 1941, almost all players saw action on both sides of the ball. World War II changed that. From 1941 through 1952, colleges had difficulty finding players, so the rules committee decided to permit a substitute to enter the game "at any time."

When Fritz Crisler, the coach at Michigan, was faced with using freshmen against a seasoned Army team in 1945, he came up with an idea.

"I asked myself, 'How are our poor, spindly legged freshmen going to stand up against these West Pointers all afternoon?'"

Crisler chose his best defensive players and told them, "When we lose the ball, you fellows automatically go in."

To his offensive men, he said, "When we regain possession, you fellows automatically go in."

They lost the game 28–7, but Crisler had started something revolutionary. The Army coach, Red Blaik, used the military word platoon for what he observed. It caught on.

From 1946 to 1950, Blaik's two-platoon teams at Army finished second twice in the AP poll and never lower than 11th.

In 1953, for financial reasons, the NCAA changed the rules to favor the one-platoon system. It allowed only one player to be substituted between plays. That caused a huge controversy among the nation's coaches. Those against the one-platoon system stated that the rule meant fewer players get to participate; less sophistication; more injuries; less fan interest; and they felt it was a move backward. Those in support of it said it was less expensive, simplified the playbooks, and focused on the fundamentals.

In 1958, LSU coach Paul Dietzel conceived of using three platoons of 11 players each to keep them from getting fatigued. The second-string defensive unit, named the Chinese Bandits, consisted of the more aggressive players. The system worked and LSU went undefeated.

After the 1964 season, the NCAA allowed an unlimited number of player substitutions. Teams could now form offensive and defensive units as well as special teams.

Today, everything's gotten bigger: the complexity of the rules, the audience, the money involved, the size of the conferences, and the players' weights have changed. Players no longer need more than a single skill to earn a starting spot.

Yet some players would love to play on both sides of the ball.

In 1996, Deion Sanders became the NFL's first full-time two-way starter since Bednarik. Sanders did it for Dallas; Michael Irvin had a five-game suspension, which resulted in Sanders being a full-time wide receiver even as he kept his full-time job at cornerback.

Against the Chicago Bears, Sanders had a solid two-way game. He was on the field for 108 of 123 plays from scrimmage: 57 on offense, 51 on defense. He caught nine passes, was avoided by the Bears on defense, and the defending Super Bowl champion Cowboys lost 22–6.

In 1981, Roy Green of the St. Louis Cardinals played both ways briefly, mostly as a wide receiver and played one year as a cornerback .

Some other iron men who graced the early stages of professional football:

- Pudge Heffelfinger, guard and defensive tackle.

- Jim Thorpe, halfback, defensive back, and drop kicker.

- Red Grange, halfback and defensive back.

- Don Hutson, split end, safety, and kicker.

- Sammy Baugh, quarterback, tailback, defensive back, and punter.

- Charlie Trippi, quarterback, halfback, punter, and return specialist.

- Mike Furrey, wide receiver and safety.

All except Heffelfinger and Furrey are in the Pro Football Hall of Fame.

Deion Sanders was on the field for 108 of 123 plays from scrimmage: 57 on offense, 51 on defense.

Eddie Robinson

Taking Black College Football to the World Stage

Eddie Robinson needed to be somewhat of a miracle worker.

In 1941, he was head football coach, basketball coach, and baseball coach at a teacher's college, Louisiana Negro Normal and Industrial Institute, later named Grambling State. Robinson had no paid assistants, no groundskeepers, no trainers, little in the way of equipment, and his monthly pay was $63.75.

NO. **40**

When he first arrived, an atmosphere of failure hung over the campus. Robinson was beset with indecision and doubt. He liked to recall, "We didn't have much to look ahead to, but even less to look back on."

Robinson had been a star quarterback at Leland College under Reuben S. Turner, a Baptist preacher who steered Robinson toward a coaching career. In his first season, Robinson's football team got off to a rocky start. He then took command and dismissed some of the players he felt weren't living up to expectations. His next year, his team went 9-0 to start a new era at Grambling.

Robinson, the son of a cotton sharecropper, knew the value of education. Neither of his parents graduated from high school. "The first thing he'd do," said Fred Hobdy, a guard at Grambling, "he'd assemble the players, tell them they had to get their education, had to get more out of this than football."

Even when players had completed their eligibility, he'd get them back in school and make sure they graduated.

As for his football teams, there was an ongoing struggle. Robinson would fix sandwiches for road trips because his players could not eat in the "White Only" restaurants in

Grambling State Tigers head coach Eddie Robinson during the 1995 season

the South. He lined the field, taped ankles, took the injured to the hospital, and made sure his players kept up with their studies. He even wrote the game stories.

He never gave up on his players.

"A daddy pulled my best running backs off our team and said they couldn't play anymore because they had to pick cotton," Robinson said. "So I got all the boys on the team, we went out there to pick cotton." When the crop was in, the players rejoined the team and won championships.

Robinson was putting together winning seasons, but the school to the north, Southern University, the "Harvard" of the black southern colleges, looked down upon its rural neighbor.

"They were the big school and the most powerful in the Southwestern Athletic Conference [SWAC]," Robinson said. "It was unheard of for us to beat them. When they came to play you, you were supposed to be whipped."

In 1947 Grambling whipped Southern, the SWAC champion, 21–6. Robinson and Grambling were becoming well known, as was the Grambling-Southern rivalry, one of the best ever in college football, known as the "Bayou Classic."

Robinson started driving the team bus through the segregated South. Sometimes it was difficult finding accommodations as well as a practice field. Once in Montgomery, Alabama,

Grambling's Doug Williams became the first black quarterback to win a Super Bowl.

Grambling wasn't allowed to work out on a football field the day before the game. Robinson found an empty parking lot and practice was held there. Another time, practice was in a hotel ballroom after the team pushed aside the tables and chairs. Robinson was always creative.

Meanwhile, Robinson was not only winning but also preparing his players for the pros, and in effect, opening doors to the National Football League for black players. Paul (Tank) Younger was one of the early success stories.

In 1948 Younger was invited to a Los Angeles Rams camp. Robinson gave Younger a pep talk and kept him at Grambling after he graduated to be sure he was in the best shape of his life. "He told me, 'Tank, you have to make the team. If you don't make it, they will say they took the best player from a black school and he couldn't make it and there's no telling when another player from a black school will get a chance.'"

By then, Grambling's football program was receiving national acclaim. Younger signed with the Rams. He became the first player from a historically black college to be taken in the NFL draft.

Robinson sent more than 200 players to the NFL and other professional leagues. Grambling's Doug Williams became the first black quarterback to win a Super Bowl when he led the Washington Redskins over the Denver Broncos, 42–10, in Super Bowl XXII. Williams played one of the greatest games in Super Bowl history, passing for 340 yards and four touchdowns to win the Most Valuable Player trophy.

Grambling was among several schools—such as Tennessee State and Jackson State, which produced Hall of Famer Walter Payton—at the center of the black football universe. While social change was happening in America in the 1960s and there were more openings for black football players in the National Football League, Robinson found it difficult to dominate in the recruiting game in a more fully integrated college environment.

"What it did do was take away the opportunity for a lot of kids to become superstars," said Robinson. "There were more guys sitting on benches in the Southeastern Conference who could be stars anyplace else."

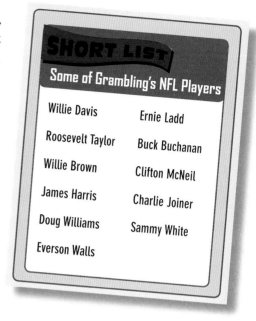

SHORT LIST

Some of Grambling's NFL Players

Willie Davis

Roosevelt Taylor

Willie Brown

James Harris

Doug Williams

Everson Walls

Ernie Ladd

Buck Buchanan

Clifton McNeil

Charlie Joiner

Sammy White

Robinson won 17 SWAC titles and had only eight losing seasons in 57 while compiling a 408-165-15 record.

"Eddie Robinson was a role model and a pacesetter," said Jesse Jackson, a quarterback at North Carolina A&T University in the 1960s. "He took black college football to the big stadiums nationally and internationally. The Grambling Tigers' football team and marching band became a worldwide frame of reference."

Robinson took over the Grambling athletic program at a time when racism ruled America and came out on top.

Sid Gillman

The Passing Game Wizard Who Created the Modern Offense

Bill Walsh said it. So did Don Coryell and Jon Gruden.

Sid Gillman was the godfather of the modern offense.

That's lofty praise from three of the greatest offensive minds to work an NFL sideline. Here's more from Raiders owner Al Davis, who knew a few things about scoring touchdowns and winning football games.

"He was way ahead of his time in organization, in the passing game, and offensive football," Davis told The Associated Press upon Gillman's death in 2003. "In the '60s, the passing game was not yet really developed. At the advent of the AFL (in 1960), certainly the Chargers were the flagship for all teams to follow, all teams to emulate."

NO. **41**

After five seasons coaching with the generally underskilled Rams, Gillman headed to the new AFL in 1960 with the Los Angeles Chargers. They moved to San Diego the next year, and he led the team to five AFL championship games, winning the title in 1963. Gillman also served as head coach of the Houston Oilers, as an assistant with the Cowboys, Bears, and Eagles, and the L.A. Express of the USFL. He was the first man to coach teams to division titles in the AFL and NFL.

In 1981 he made Super Bowl XV with Philadelphia as offensive coordinator for Dick Vermeil. "I had a certain lack of depth in my background in regard to the passing game," Vermeil told the *New York Times* in '81. "That is why I hired Sid two years ago."

Gillman immediately made a huge difference.

"Until Sid got here," quarterback Ron Jaworski said, "we were a basic formation team, we were predictable. But now we line up in different formations—a slot, a slot split, doubles, deuces. You name it, we've got it. And he is responsible."

San Diego Chargers head coach Sid Gillman on the sideline

AUDIBLE

On the Big Money Plays

"The big play comes with the pass. God bless those runners because they get you the first down, give you ball control and keep your defense off the field. But if you want to ring the cash register, you have to pass." —*Sid Gillman*

For more than five decades, professional teams have tried to replicate what Gillman created in San Diego: spreading out receivers and backs; challenging defenses deep; a route tree for wideouts with variations that gave the receivers options while giving defensive backs fits.

These tactics continue to dominate the pro and college game today.

For Gillman, no coaching tool was more effective than game film. While he didn't originate the use of it for scouting opponents—and critiquing his own team—he so refined breaking down film that coaches and quarterbacks from everywhere would consult Gillman on techniques for analyzing what was on the screen.

And to think Gillman almost couldn't afford to buy a projector when he first stepped into coaching.

Gillman played end at Ohio State and recognized very soon after saying goodbye to Columbus that he was not built for playing in the pros. Bronko Nagurski convinced Gillman of that with a monstrous tackle in the College All-Star Game of 1934.

He took a job at Denison University, where he saw an ad for a 35-millimeter projector at a cost of $35. "We can't afford that," his wife, Esther, told him. "He says, 'I have to have this.' That was the beginning. He would come home, we would put up a white sheet on the wall, Sid would show me these films."

As Gillman worked his way up the coaching ladder, both college and pro football had yet to fully discover the benefits of the passing game he so vehemently espoused. Football was a running game on offense, a power game on defense. Consider that in 1954, the year before Gillman took over the Rams, the leader in receptions was the Rams' Bob Boyd with 53 in 12 games.

When the wild-and-wooly AFL came along in 1960, though, the landscape changed. So did the airways. No one was more of a catalyst for that change than Gillman.

"I believe that was the beginning of the West Coast offense, what we had in San Diego," said Hall of Fame receiver Lance Alworth. "Sid was the inventor of it, he started it all. He had an innovative way of looking at it, and once he put the system together and John (Hadl) learned how to run it, we knew we could score points.

"It was fun to play, it was totally different than anything I had played in college. I loved to catch the football and run with it and this gave me the opportunity to do what I did best and enjoyed the most."

Gillman's head coaching record of 122-99-7 wasn't that gaudy. His impact on the game was undeniably palpable, though, and Gillman was inducted into the Pro Football Hall of Fame in 1983.

It seems fitting that three dynamic offensive weapons went in that year, too: Sonny Jurgensen, Bobby Mitchell, and Paul Warfield.

When Gillman made the shrine, he was at a function on Super Bowl Sunday in Atlantic City during which many other Hall of Famers were feted. He admitted to feeling out of place.

And then . . .

"I was sitting, signing autographs and the game was coming on," Gillman told The Associated Press. "A public relations man comes over and says, 'There's someone for you on the telephone.' I said to tell him he'll have to call back later.

"Five minutes later, there was another call. The PR man returned and said, 'You have to answer the phone.' I thought that it must be very important, with the Super Bowl starting and all.

"I answer the phone and a guy says, 'Congratulations.' I say, 'For what?'"

For being selected to the Hall.

"I just about died," he said. "I had no idea they were selecting, or that I was being considered."

Through the years, Gillman would spot his former assistant coaches leading other teams, and he would swell with pride.

It was unfathomable that he had not previously been more seriously considered. And through the years, Gillman would spot his former assistant coaches leading other teams, and he would swell with pride, whether it was Chuck Noll, the first coach to lead a franchise to four Super Bowl crowns, or a position coach feverishly working his trade.

"All I know is that when you look over at the coaches on the other sideline and all you see are guys who either coached with you or played for you, then you know it's time to get out," he once told the *New York Times*. "I learned from everybody whose staff I was on. You always learn something."

Dick LeBeau and the Zone Blitz

Seemingly Chaotic Defenses Confuse Offenses

Dick LeBeau made the Pro Football Hall of Fame because of his performances as a defensive back with the Detroit Lions for 14 seasons.

But it wasn't in the secondary where LeBeau truly became an NFL game changer. It was on the sideline and in the coaching booth.

Few defensive coordinators have had the effect on pro football of LeBeau. The Steelers went to the Super Bowl in the 1995 season, his first as coordinator in Pittsburgh after eight years with the Bengals. He spent only two years in the Steel City before returning to Cincinnati, where he was fired in 2002 after three seasons as head coach. LeBeau brought the Steel Curtain back to Pittsburgh in 2004; the Steelers ranked first in overall defense in five of his 11 seasons on the job, when their home was dubbed "Blitzburgh."

LeBeau's greatest contribution, copied by every NFL club, most college teams, and even down to the high school level, was the zone blitz.

The blitz has existed for decades, usually defined as an extra defender coming from the linebacker or backfield positions to rush the passer. The idea is simple: send more guys than the offense can block, forcing the passer to get rid of the ball prematurely, getting a backfield tackle on a runner, or, even better, sacking the quarterback.

Very little about the zone blitz is simple. Just ask Baltimore QB Joe Flacco, who faced LeBeau and the Steelers at least twice a season in each of his first seven years as a Raven.

The Dick LeBeau-inspired Pittsburgh Steelers defense

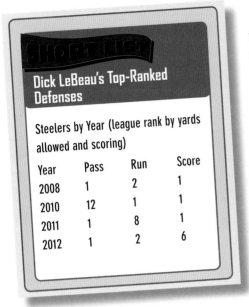

SHORTLIST

Dick LeBeau's Top-Ranked Defenses

Steelers by Year (league rank by yards allowed and scoring)

Year	Pass	Run	Score
2008	1	2	1
2010	12	1	1
2011	1	8	1
2012	1	2	6

"The biggest thing over there has been the players that they have and their ability to really sit there and run it and do the amount of things that he asks them to do," Flacco told the *Baltimore Sun*. "I don't know if his call sheet is very long or elaborate or anything like that, but he can come up with some things that are tough for offenses, and those guys are very good at doing what he wants and operating it."

Here's what LeBeau wanted: a confused offense being dominated by what looks like a chaotic defense, yet is a very precise scheme.

LeBeau was first tutored by then–Louisiana State head coach Bill Arnsparger in the ways of the blitz. Arnsparger had been a terrific defensive coordinator in the pros, putting together the No-Name Defense in Miami that won two Super Bowls, including in the undefeated 1972 season. LeBeau's boss in Cincinnati at the time, Sam Wyche, wanted an aggressive and unpredictable defense.

LeBeau delivered with a 3-4 alignment in which just about anybody could be coming at any time. Fully recognizing the importance of what he called a "safe blitz" in which his secondary was protected from one-on-one coverages nearly everywhere, he installed a variety of rushes in which any combination of the four linebackers might rush the passer. But any of the linemen might drop back into short coverage.

Those 1984 Bengals, not overflowing with defensive talent, might line up in a 3-4-4, then a 4-1-6, then a 5-1-5—anything to plant doubt in the enemy play callers and quarterbacks.

When LeBeau got to Pittsburgh in 1991, he coached defensive backs under coordinator Dom Capers. By 1995, when he became defensive coordinator, he had the horses to implement any and every scheme. With defensive backs Darren Perry, Willie Williams, and Carnell Lake—Hall of Famer Rod Woodson was injured that AFC championship season—and, especially, linebackers Greg Lloyd, Kevin Greene, and Chad Brown, LeBeau could bring to bear pretty much anything he could dream up.

He came up with enough that Greene had nine sacks, defensive end Ray Seals had eight and a half, and the team managed 42. Many came when blockers were uncertain who was their responsibility, and someone came free to plaster the quarterback. Eleven Steelers had sacks that season.

"The good thing about Dick, he tries to envision what's the less stress put on the DBs, because a lot of times when you see a lot of these exotic blitzes, they're unsound in the secondary . . . they can get beat," Woodson told NFL.com. "I think the one thing Dick tries to do is to eliminate that as best possible."

Although LeBeau returned to Cincinnati and was head coach for almost three years (the Bengals went 12-23), the Steelers welcomed him back in 2004, when they went 15-1 despite playing a rookie QB, Ben Roethlisberger. For the next decade, it was open season on opposing offenses in Blitzburgh.

LeBeau's refinements included changing coverages despite employing the zone blitzes. At times, he'd order man coverage, or even matchup man in which the routes being run determined which defender went where. The receivers make their first moves and the defenders pick them up in man coverage.

There was more, of course. With LeBeau's active and creative mind, there always was more.

He might put a safety or cornerback in the box without disguising the player's intention of rushing the quarterback, who then had to find his hot receiver. Trouble was, the heat would reach the QB before he could get off a pass.

Then there was the fire zone, a blitz that has burned through the NFL in the last decade or so. Basically, it's a five-man rush with three pass defenders handling deep coverage and three dealing with underneath patterns. Problem is figuring out who is coming and who is dropping back. And where.

"He's always on the cutting edge of creating new things," said Rex Ryan, himself a defensive mastermind who had some epic matchups with LeBeau. "His players play extremely hard for him. They have great trust in him."

Why not? While everywhere around them, the NFL game tilted toward wide-open attacks and plenty of high scoring, LeBeau was coming up with answers. That's why Tennessee hired him at age 77 after he parted with the Steelers in 2015.

For the next decade, it was open season on opposing offenses in Blitzburgh.

"I always felt that we contributed greatly to the development of the run-and-shoot offense," LeBeau told Grantland.com. "Teams were just looking for quicker and quicker ways to attack, to the point where it might not even matter where the pressure was coming from."

The pressure was coming from a LeBeau defense. Always.

Deacon Jones

The Man Who Coined the Term "Sack"

One fitting measure of a man's greatness is what his peers say about him.

Another and even more impressive measure is what those who followed him—and either didn't know him or never saw him perform—say about him.

For David "Deacon" Jones, the tributes began while he was terrorizing the NFL as the most fearsome of the Los Angeles Rams' Fearsome Foursome defensive front. They have never stopped.

To everyone, Deacon Jones was "The Sackmaster." Heck, he even coined the term. "You know, like you sack a city," he explained. "Devastate it."

Unfortunately, Jones never got the credit so many others have received because the NFL didn't tally sacks as an official statistic until 1982, eight years after Jones

NO. 43

knocked down his last quarterback. Not that numbers could define someone like Jones, whose impact on the game was so profound that he entered the Pro Football Hall of Fame with virtual unanimous approval from the voters in 1980.

"Deacon Jones has been the most inspirational person in my football career," fellow Hall of Famer Jack Youngblood said.

Added Bruce Smith, the career sacks leader, while appearing on NFL Network after Jones's death in 2013: "Not only to coin the term sack, but just his personality of being a defensive lineman; his charisma and his presence. When he walked into the room, he commanded respect, whether it was on the playing field or [for] his choice of words."

And this from current Rams defensive end Chris Long: "The thing we've got to remember being players in this era is to really respect the game 'back when,' because those guys could really play. Deacon Jones is a perfect example. This whole league and everybody in this game should honor the past and the players who played in that era. Those guys paved the way for us."

Los Angeles Rams defensive tackle Deacon Jones pressures
Baltimore Colts quarterback Johnny Unitas, October 15, 1967.

On a Name to Remember

"No one would remember a player named David Jones—there are a thousand David Joneses in the phone book. I picked out Deacon because it has a religious connotation and it would be remembered in the violent pro football world. When the Rams sent out my player questionnaire, I simply listed my name as Deacon Jones. From then on, that's what I was." —*David "Deacon" Jones*

AUDIBLE

Jones was the main prototypet of the modern pass-rushing defensive lineman. Using a head slap that eventually was banned from the game, Jones could knock a blocker off-balance or, even more profoundly, knock him silly. His combination of strength, speed, size (6'5", 272, large in the 1960s and 70s), guile, and guts at times made Jones unblockable.

That head slap was just part of his repertoire. Before Jones came along, most defensive ends used a bull rush or a speed rush. Few could combine both effectively, not even the many Hall of Famers who preceded Jones in the NFL.

But the Deacon did his damage with a variety of maneuvers. Once the Rams had put together the Fearsome Foursome that also included fellow Hall of Famer Merlin Olsen, Rosey Grier, and Lamar Lundy, the pass rushers would use stunts to get into the backfield. Jones might loop inside one of the defensive tackles, forcing a matchup with a guard or even a center—almost a guaranteed mismatch.

His long arms helped Jones keep blockers at a safe distance, and one of his coaches, George Allen, felt Jones was a perfect special teamer with his long reach and intimidating persona.

Jones was durable. Today, when many top sack threats are given plays or even entire series off to keep them fresh, Jones might not fit in. He wanted, expected—insisted—on being on the field, play after play.

From 1961, when he was drafted in the 14th round out of traditionally black Mississippi Valley State, until 1970, Jones played in every game. He missed suiting up only five times in his 14 pro seasons.

A five-time All-Pro despite never winning a championship, Jones was the very embodiment of the sack. He didn't simply hit quarterbacks, he, well yeah, devastated them. By reputation alone, he made every passer nervous about dropping back. They became even more reticent to do so once they'd been run over by Jones.

Yes, the Deacon, despite his nickname, was as threatening as an athlete can be, never smiling on the field, most often scowling.

Jones didn't simply hit quarterbacks, he devastated them.

He also was the fulcrum of the Fearsome Foursome, the leader of a defense that perennially ranked among the NFL's stingiest. Allen, among the best defensive minds in NFL coaching history, called Jones "without doubt the greatest defensive end to play in modern day football."

"Deacon was an incredible team guy and he always wanted to win; he wanted all of us to run the race together," Grier said. "We didn't play run, we played pass, and we all came off the ball together. The whole point was to get in the backfield fast and mess everything up. They couldn't stop the Fearsome Foursome—we made a great contribution to the game of football."

Jones wasn't just larger than life on the field. His outspokenness away from the game was noteworthy, too. He once told ESPN: "I'm probably the toughest (expletive) here. Ain't no question about that with me. . . . I ain't got no marks on me, so I've got to be the baddest dude I know of."

Described by a journalist as a famous football player, he produced that on-field scowl and answered: "Know the difference between famous and great."

Asked a politically touchy question, Jones responded: "A nation that spends billions to fix international problems will not have much left over for the victims of tornadoes in Oklahoma."

He even tried his hand at acting, appearing in the 1978 film *Heaven Can Wait*, starring Warren Beatty, as well as several television shows. Had they ever made a TV series about Jones's life, it could have had only one title: *The Sackmaster*.

Jim Parker

The Mobile Immovable Object

If only there was a steady stream of highlights of Jim Parker, the Sack Preventer, blocking Deacon Jones, the Sackmaster, NFL Network could have a classic series on its hands.

Sure, it's cliched, but the name of the program that best fits: "Irresistible Force vs. Immovable Object."

Actually, Parker wasn't immovable at all—except when someone was trying to get past him to find the ball carrier or passer. He was the most mobile of offensive linemen in an era (1957–1967) when mobility wasn't at a premium. Parker changed the way offensive tackles played, and the way they were regarded. Weeb Ewbank, his coach during championship seasons in Baltimore in 1958 and '59—and like Parker a Pro Football Hall of Fame member—once said that Parker "made it smart for teams to go find (offensive) linemen in the draft."

NO. 44

At 6'3", 273 pounds, Parker would be considered minuscule by today's offensive line standards. He was huge for his day. The biggest player drafted by Baltimore at the time, "he blocked out the sun," former Colts GM Ernie Accorsi said.

At Ohio State, he was a consensus All-American and the first African-American Outland Trophy winner. He even played defense for the Buckeyes, and with the Colts, for whom he made eight straight All-Pro teams, Parker was the perfect blocker: strong, smart, mobile, relentless.

"Physically, Jim was in a class by himself," Ohio State's legendary coach Woody Hayes said while introducing Parker at his Hall of Fame induction. "Attitude-wise, he was even greater. You only had to tell him once."

Selected eighth overall in the 1957 draft, Parker was the first full-time offensive lineman enshrined in Canton. He played both tackle and guard for the Colts, making some All-Pro squads at both positions in 1962. Parker protected John Unitas in the passing game,

Baltimore Colts tackle Jim Parker was 6'3" and 273 pounds—
small by current standards but huge for his day.

and dominated defenders when Baltimore ran the ball, mostly with Lenny Moore. His All-Pro honors came at tackle from 1958 to 1961, and at guard the next four seasons.

Parker came into the pros as a road grader, someone who would plow over and through opponents in the ground attack that was prevalent in the Big Ten—and particularly under Hayes at Ohio State. The first lesson when he got to Baltimore was simple.

"It didn't take me long to learn the one big rule," Parker was quoted on the Hall of Fame website. "'Just keep them away from John,' Coach Ewbank told me at my first practice: 'You can be the most unpopular man on the team if the quarterback gets hurt.' I couldn't forget that!"

He never did, even though Parker prided himself just as much on clearing a path for Moore, Alan Ameche, and other runners.

"As Johnny's protector, Jim was second to none," Moore, another Hall of Famer, told the *Baltimore Sun*. "If Jim got through the line, I'd be right on his hip because I knew he'd clear out the area."

Although Parker never officially was credited with inventing the term, his teammates insisted he was the king of the pancake.

Although Parker never officially was credited with inventing the term, his teammates insisted he was the king of the pancake.

"He was a legitimate starter from the first day of training camp," Colts center Buzz Nutter told the *Sun*. "About twice a game, Parker would absolutely pancake a linebacker, running over him like a big elephant. The guy would disappear like he'd been driven right into the ground."

But his game hardly was all power, although his strength and ability to anchor made the move to guard in the second half of Parker's career a smooth one. Parker's foot skills were uncommon, and once he'd established himself in the pros, other teams would send their scouts to college games looking for agile blockers, not just behemoths.

Eventually, the prototypical offensive lineman would combine movement with muscle and bulk. Nowadays, virtually every guy in the trenches, colleges and the NFL, weighs more than 300 pounds and is light on his feet.

Parker was the first.

"I used to think that I could outmaneuver any big tackle, but that Parker can stay with anybody," Andy Robustelli, yet another Hall of Famer who was tamed by Parker, told the Coffin Corner. "He sure could move with me. The only way you can beat him is to make him move his head. But he is too strong and too good and too smart to do that."

Parker preferred the matchups with the bigger defensive tackles that came with the switch to guard. He knew his skill set provided an awful matchup for them. "That is one thing I liked about playing guard," Parker said. "The tackles were bigger and usually not as agile as the ends. I liked the big guys. Speed boys gave me trouble. I also noticed that the guard's blocking space was comparatively limited. Blocking a defensive end meant more movement. The end had lots of space outside to roam."

Perhaps, but not often against Parker.

After playing in 139 straight games, Parker injured his knee in 1967. He retired because he knew he couldn't play at the same nonpareil level he'd performed at for a decade. Colts coach Don Shula called it "maybe the most unselfish act in sports history" because the Colts were unbeaten (10-0-2) and likely headed for the playoffs.

"I can't help the team," Parker said, "and I won't deprive 40 guys of their big chance."

Of course, Parker already had helped the Colts far more than anyone could have asked.

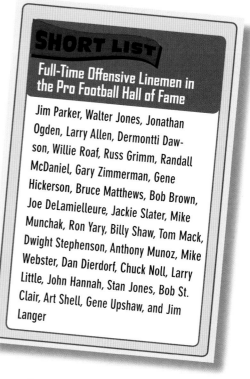

SHORT LIST

Full-Time Offensive Linemen in the Pro Football Hall of Fame

Jim Parker, Walter Jones, Jonathan Ogden, Larry Allen, Dermontti Dawson, Willie Roaf, Russ Grimm, Randall McDaniel, Gary Zimmerman, Gene Hickerson, Bruce Matthews, Bob Brown, Joe DeLamielleure, Jackie Slater, Mike Munchak, Ron Yary, Billy Shaw, Tom Mack, Dwight Stephenson, Anthony Munoz, Mike Webster, Dan Dierdorf, Chuck Noll, Larry Little, John Hannah, Stan Jones, Bob St. Clair, Art Shell, Gene Upshaw, and Jim Langer

As for those battles with the Deacon, well, Jones naturally claims they were one-sided in his favor. "One of them wouldn't do against me," he told ESPN.com when asked about offensive linemen. "You should be asking me who were the toughest 'two' linemen, or what was the toughest combination or the toughest team—because you'd definitely have to bring more than one when you come at me. If you just bring one, I'm going to kill somebody."

Perhaps somebody. But definitely not Jim Parker.

Rutgers vs. Princeton, 1869

An Odd Game in New Jersey Kicks Off American Football

True or false: College football started in America when Rutgers hosted Princeton in 1869.

True, if you believe Rutgers. False, if you believe Tufts University, which has its own side of the story.

The long-held belief that Rutgers' 6–4 victory over Princeton on November 6, 1869, was the birth of the sport is being challenged by a Tufts official who believes his school actually played the first game, against Harvard in 1875.

NO. **45**

"We're not trying to displace anybody," Rocky Carzo, former coach and athletic director at Tufts, told the *Boston Globe*. "It's just part of being in the academic business is being in quest for the truth.

"This is the first game between two U.S. colleges playing rules as we really know football. From our standpoint, it's indisputable."

Carzo goes further, citing the Harvard-McGill game of that same year as the first game between North American colleges, and Tufts-Harvard as the first between American-based colleges.

Back to 1869:

With Rutgers and Princeton only 22 miles apart, it was natural that a rivalry would develop. A three-game football series was scheduled in the 1869 season. Princeton had routed Rutgers 40–2 in baseball and Rutgers longed for revenge on the football field. The game would be played on a plot of land now called College Field in New Brunswick, New Jersey.

The first ever intercollegiate football game between Princeton and Rutgers in November 1869

On Seeing Stars at Football's Other "First" Game—June 4, 1875, Tufts vs. Harvard

"The play opened briskly and [before] long five or six Tufts men found themselves laid on their back so violently that they imagined it was evening, by the stars they saw. They soon repaid the compliment, however." —Boston Daily Globe

AUDIBLE

The first game was won by Rutgers and the second by Princeton before the third was canceled by protests from the faculties of both institutions. The professors had complained that football was interfering with the students' studies.

The Rutgers-Princeton game, called "foot-ball" by the student newspaper, the *Targum*, resembled a combination of rugby and soccer, with touchdowns worth one point. It was played with 25 men a side on a field roughly 120 yards by 75, with goalposts 24 feet apart. The ball was round and made of rubber, according to the Rutgers student newspaper. Throwing and carrying the ball was against the rules. The ball was only advanced by kicking and batting it with hands, feet, sides, and heads.

About 100 spectators showed up for the mid-afternoon contest. "Instead of kaleidoscopic colors and highly protective equipment, a few Rutgers players wore scarlet turbans and one man sported a bright red jersey, prophetic of the color later to be adopted by the college," the *New York Times* said.

With no uniforms, the players stripped off their hats, coats, and vests and bound their suspenders around the waistbands of their trousers.

Twelve players from each team moved around the field as the offense; two players stayed near the opponent's goal; and 11 players stayed in their own end on defense. The game was "replete with surprises, strategy, prodigies of determination and physical prowess," to use the words of one of the players.

The spectators were sitting on a fence chanting "college cheers and songs, and when either side kicked, the spectators yelled with complete abandon," reported the *New York Times* on November 6, 1929.

The Rutgers men had evolved a play that became famous a few years later as "the flying wedge," where the runner is protected by a moving "V" or a "flying wedge" of players. Stephan G. Gano, class of '71, and George R. Dixon, '73, combined to score the first tally.

"Next period Rutgers bucked, or received the ball, hoping to repeat the flying wedge," wrote John W. Herbert, Rutgers '72, who was one of the players. The play was broken up time and again by the Tigers' J. E. Michael, '71, known to his teammates as "Big Mike."

First team to score six goals won the game, the rules stated. Both teams alternated at making goals in the early going.

The seventh goal featured a misplay by one of the excited Rutgers players, who lost direction and kicked the ball toward his own team's goal. The kick was blocked, but Princeton made use of it by scoring into the Rutgers goal to tie the game at four goals apiece.

The seventh goal featured a misplay by one of the excited Rutgers players, who lost direction and kicked the ball toward his own team's goal.

At that tie score, Rutgers captain William J. Leggett told his men to keep the ball low, less handy to the taller Princeton players, and Rutgers used that strategy to win, 6–4. Princeton won the second game, 8–0.

Meanwhile, Ivy League schools soon joined Rutgers and Princeton in playing this new brand of football. Princeton dominated football in the 1800s and was considered the national champion more than 10 times. Harvard and Yale were also recognized as national powers.

Today, the signs at High Point Solutions Stadium in Piscataway, New Jersey, read: The Birthplace of College Football.

But is Rutgers the birthplace of college football? Tufts University would not agree and would claim it is the legitimate site for the first intercollegiate football game in America. That contest was played under the "Boston rules," more central to the football style of the day in 1875 and more closely resembling the modern game.

Proponents arguing for the Tufts-Harvard game point to the Rutgers-Princeton contest as a European version that should take a back seat to Harvard-Tufts.

Like the Rutgers-Princeton game, the contest between Tufts and Harvard six years later on June 4, 1875, was brutal from the start.

For the record, Tufts scored the game's only touchdown when N. L. Campbell carried the ball over the goal line. That would have been illegal if played within the rules used in the Rutgers-Princeton game, which outlawed picking up and running with the ball.

Nevertheless, the Rutgers-Princeton clash of '69 remains the generally accepted start of football in America, the evolutionary dawn.

Globalization

Following the Footsteps of Soccer, That "Other" Football

The NFL is not satisfied with having conquered America, entrenching itself as the unquestioned No. 1 sport in this country. Oh no, there are many other regions to rule—or at least to make inroads.

The checklist stretches from neighboring Canada and Mexico, where many fans would welcome more meaningful games, to Europe and South America. In such far-flung places as Japan, China, South Korea, and Australia, the league's marketing arm is reaching out to educate and entice new fans, even though there's virtually no chance any matches will be played there.

NO. 46

As long as the NFL is creating a following (read: merchandise partners and customers, and social media users) across the globe, the length of its tentacles will expand.

"There is a great desire and passion for our game in the U.K.," Commissioner Roger Goodell has said countless times. "We're certainly interested in anywhere that there's a hunger for football."

He means American football, of course; the NFL isn't likely to ever challenge the other football (soccer, *futbol*) for world supremacy. No matter: The niche the NFL has carved for itself is large, strong, and very lucrative.

The league began playing abroad in 1950, with the first 10 preseason contests staged in Canada. Tokyo hosted the first of its 13 exhibition games in 1976 and Mexico City got the first of its six in '78. Australia, Sweden, Germany, Spain, and Ireland also have had preseason matches.

Those games, 58 in all, worked well enough to whet the appetite—or at least entertain the locals with something different, if slightly incomprehensible to them. The true

Miami against Oakland in London

breakthrough internationally came in 2005 when the Cardinals played a regular-season home game in Azteca Stadium in Mexico City against the 49ers. Arizona's 31–14 victory was witnessed by 103,467 aficionados.

"I think this game lets the fans here in Mexico, the athletes here in Mexico and businesses and everybody else know that we're for real," Commissioner Paul Tagliabue said that October. "It was an element of legitimacy."

Somewhat. But the NFL didn't go back to Mexico in the next decade, instead turning its attention to England (heavily) and to Canada (temporarily).

The Canadian series of regular-season home games in Toronto that the Bills played from 2008 to 2013 were designed not to test a future franchise market but to expand the team's popularity and fan base beyond Buffalo. It flopped.

But London? Ah, London.

The first major step came when Miami switched a home game to Wembley Stadium against the Giants in 2007. The turf was a slippery mess and New York won a less-than-artistic 13–10 verdict. But the stands were full.

Back the league went once a season through 2012, and the response was just as encouraging. Hours after tickets went on sale they were gobbled up.

"What we're really trying to accomplish is build the popularity and the fan base of the sport on an ongoing basis," said NFL vice president of international Mark Waller. "And so the approach that we've taken is a focus on 'Let's build out this, let's see how many people love the game, see how much love they have.'"

The NFL was sold on London, and the Brits appeared to be sold on American football.

Plenty, apparently. The league upped the number of London matches to two in 2013, three in 2014 and '15. As long as the NFL can find franchises willing to surrender a true home game to be the host in England, those games will happen.

An added benefit for the NFL: the threat, whether real or imagined, that the league had designs on relocating across the pond should it find that logical (and profitable).

Regardless, the NFL was sold on London, and the Brits appeared to be sold on the NFL.

"The NFL has a huge fan base here," British culture secretary Sajid Javid told The Associated Press. "I hope it will become a second home for American football."

Waller, who is a Brit, could see a franchise landing in London, just not for a while. "There is no value to anybody putting a team here and finding the rigors of the season do not allow it to compete at the highest level," Waller said in 2014. "So that's the work we are going to do. That's probably a five-year piece of work."

SHORT LIST

Some of the NFL Exhibition Games Played Outside of the United States

1988	July 31	Miami Dolphins	27–21	San Francisco 49ers	Wembley Stadium	London	United Kingdom
1988	August 14	Minnesota Vikings	28–21	Chicago Bears	Ullevi Stadium	Goteborg	Sweden
1994	July 31	Los Angeles Raiders	25–22 (OT)	Denver Broncos	Estadi Olimpic	Barcelona	Spain
1994	August 7	Minnesota Vikings	17–9	Kansas City Chiefs	Tokyo Dome	Tokyo	Japan
1999	August 8	Denver Broncos	20–17	San Diego Chargers	Stadium Australia	Sydney	Australia
2002	August 3	Washington Redskins	38–7	San Francisco 49ers	Osaka Dome	Osaka	Japan

Meanwhile, the league is exploring other territories in its globalization project. Among the most interested locales, aside from Mexico, are Germany and Brazil. Neither of those soccer powers—Brazil owns a record five World Cup titles and Germany has four—is seeking a permanent franchise. Both displayed interest in staging games to Goodell and Waller.

"As for where we go next? We started the work that really looks at Germany, Mexico, potentially Brazil," Waller said in early 2015. "Those are probably the three markets where we are most likely to play an international series game next, outside of the U.K.

"That doesn't mean we are not looking at what more could we do to grow other aspects of what we do regardless of whether we play games in a market. For an example, in Germany, can we get better free-to-air media coverage for our season?"

A unique concept was presented to the NFL in 2015 by Brazilian sports officials, who believe they have become a substantial sports player after hosting the 2014 World Cup and the 2016 Summer Olympics in Rio de Janeiro. They want the Pro Bowl.

"Specifically to the Pro Bowl, our thinking is if you have a new market that is starting to become interested, the Pro Bowl might be a very good way for fans to get more acquainted with the NFL," Waller said. "Lots of star players are playing in the game, from probably all 32 teams as well, in a much more relaxed and informal, helmets-off atmosphere for a lot of the time."

Considering its track record, the NFL will find a way to get it done.

Pete Gogolak

The Father of Soccer-Style Placekicking

One of the biggest changes in football concerned the foot.

Makes sense.

Not quite so logical was the catalyst for that change, a Hungarian soccer player named Pete Gogolak.

Until Gogolak came along in the early 1960s, placekicking was a straight-ahead proposition. Some of the great kickers of the day, such as Lou Groza and Pat Summerall, faced the goalposts, stepped forward, and let it fly.

NO. *47*

Kicking field goals and extra points also wasn't such a specialized job back then; Gogolak helped usher in the era of kicker specialization, too. Groza was also a lineman and Gino Cappelletti was a wide receiver and kicker—both became frequent Pro Bowlers.

In college, it was relatively normal that star players handled kicking duties. Notre Dame's Paul Hornung parlayed his all-around skills, which included kicking and punting, into a Heisman Trophy in 1956—the only player from a losing team to earn the honor. Hornung then became a Hall of Fame pro in Green Bay, a dynamic quadruple threat: running, passing, receiving, and kicking.

His modus operandi when booting the ball? Straight on, just like everyone else in the sport.

And then Gogolak appeared, first at Cornell, then with the Buffalo Bills of the AFL. A sidewinder. A soccer-style placekicker who took two steps back from the holder, then three steps to the side.

"What the —?" traditionalists said, rubbing their eyes, or simply laughing out loud at the absurdity of Gogolak's methods. Except for one thing: Gogolak was good, so good, in fact, that nothing would ever be the same in the kicking game.

"He didn't miss," said Lou Saban, coach of the Bills when Gogolak arrived. "Kicking field goals was not such a big part of the game in 1964, but Pete made it big."

New York Giants kicker Pete Gogolak at RFK Stadium, November 29, 1970

On One of the Most Frightening Plays in the Game of Football

"The holder was always afraid, coming from the side, [that] I would kick him in the butt or kick his hands. As a matter of fact, when I played in my rookie year with the Bills, [star quarterback and future U.S. Rep.] Jack Kemp refused to hold the ball for me because of that. So, it was unusual. Since then, a lot of things have changed." —*Pete Gogolak*

AUDIBLE

Cornell might be a hotspot for doctors and engineers, but the Ivy League of that time hardly was a factory for pro football talent. Still, after Bills scout Harvey Johnson saw Gogolak boot a half-dozen bombs through the uprights, he declared, "I've seen enough," according to Gogolak. Gogolak was on his way to Buffalo, though not without many adjustments.

"I was not drafted by the NFL out of college and the Bills drafted me; I think that I was the very last draft choice," he told Northjersey.com. "Back in those days, they had no specialists. The team was 33 players and most of the time the kicker also played other positions.

"Nobody ever kicked the ball sideways and the resistance was really that nobody wanted to hold the ball because it was such a new way to kick a football." Holders were afraid of getting kicked. Gogolak made 19 of 29 field goal attempts as a rookie in Buffalo, not exactly world-shattering numbers. It must be remembered, however, that field conditions often ranged from mediocre to impassable, particularly at the dank War Memorial Stadium the Bills called home. Three of his misses were from beyond 50 yards.

Footballs in the 1960s were like most equipment used in the game—not primitive, but not close to state-of-the-art.

Buffalo won the AFL title in 1964. Gogolak was used far more the next season, leading the AFL with 46 attempts, making 28. He was voted to the league's all-star squad.

It could be argued that Gogolak's success was just as significant to the development of football as the emergence of the great early passers such as Sammy Baugh and Sid Luckman. Or the powerful middle linebackers (Ray Nitschke, Dick Butkus), masterful sacksters (Deacon Jones and Alan Page) and pass-catching tight ends (John Mackey, Mike Ditka).

In his wake came a wave of marvelous sidewinders, including Jan Stenerud, the only pure placekicker in the Pro Football Hall of Fame. After Gogolak's arrival, it became virtually impossible for a team to compete without a proficient kicker.

The only true backlash against the soccer-style guys came from the likes of throwback defensive tackle Alex Karras, as much a comic figure as a bruiser. Karras loved to mock the kickers by yelling, "I kick a touchdown, I kick a touchdown!"

In general, soccer-style kickers became accepted almost overnight in pro football. By the 1970s, it was the only manner by which field goals and extra points were kicked.

When he retired in 1974, Gogolak was the Giants' career scoring leader. Hardly the circus act many traditionalists dubbed him when he joined the Bills.

Gogolak, whose younger brother Charlie kicked for seven NFL seasons, played a leading role in the merger between the AFL and NFL when he jumped leagues, from the Bills to the Giants in 1966. So his role as a game changer came on two everlasting levels.

After Gogolak's arrival, it became virtually impossible for a team to compete without a proficient kicker.

More than 50 years since his debut at Cornell, there have been very few other innovations in kicking the football. About the most noticeable is the rugby-style punt that has been in vogue in the colleges since the 21st century began.

Hardly revolutionary.

"I think the thinking was that it might be amusing," Gogolak said of his getting a chance in pro football. "Here's a guy who kicks the ball differently. Let's give him a shot at it."

A shot heard and seen 'round the football world.

Mr. Heisman

A Coaching Vagabond Lobbies and Lobbies for the Forward Pass, and Does So Much More

Who was John Heisman?

The player/coach for whom the Heisman Trophy is named was a coaching vagabond. His ideas were radical, out of the box, and he was never afraid of controversy.

He coached at nine schools—nine—and left a trail that revolutionized football forever after.

If he had been successful in following his first career path as a lawyer, none of his football genius would have been discovered. As it was, Heisman only turned to football because poor eyesight prevented him from going into the field of law.

NO. **48**

Clemson, Georgia Tech, and Auburn were among his many stops along a widespread coaching trail. He won a National Championship at Georgia Tech in 1917, where he turned out four unbeaten teams in 16 seasons.

One of his major contributions involved the development of the forward pass. In 1895 Heisman was scouting a game between Georgia and North Carolina when something unusual happened. North Carolina's punter was about to be swamped. He didn't have time to kick the ball, so he threw it to get rid of it as quickly as possible. A teammate caught it and in the confusion ran 70 yards. Touchdown! The only one of the game. The Georgia coach yelled in protest. The rattled referee turned a blind eye to this new development and claimed not to have seen the ball thrown.

It made an impression on Heisman. Why not legalize the forward pass? The Rules Committee chair was Walter Camp, so Heisman turned to him. The answer was an emphatic *no*!

Every year Heisman presented his case, and the answer was always the same.

Georgia Tech football team, 1911, Coach John Heisman in the center row, middle

SHORT LIST

The First Five Heisman Trophy Winners

YEAR	NAME	SCHOOL	POSITION	POINTS	% OF POINTS POSSIBLE	CLASS
1935	Jay Berwanger*	Chicago	Halfback	84	43.08%	Senior
1936	Larry Kelley	Yale	End	219	36.41%	Senior
1937	Clint Frank	Yale	Halfback	524	32.89%	Senior
1938	Davey O'Brien	TCU	Quarterback	519	29.62%	Senior
1939	Nile Kinnick	Iowa	Halfback/Quarterback	651	31.00%	Senior

*First overall draft pick in the NFL draft

Finally 11 years later in 1906, with an ultimatum from President Theodore Roosevelt to clean up the violence in the game, the forward pass was legalized. The NCAA accepted Heisman's argument that passing would open up the game, and spread out contact on the field, thus cutting down on injuries.

That was only one of the innovations that Heisman was credited with bringing into the game. His improvisational skills were usually a step ahead of his coaching colleagues. Heisman was especially sharp in the offensive side of the game, and was credited with using laterals, reverses, and pulling guards on sweeps. He was the first to ask his quarterback to yell "Yup!" or "Hike!" when signaling a snap.

His bag of tricks also included the hidden-ball maneuver. One time he even pulled off the "hidden team trick." Heisman had brought his Clemson team into Atlanta to face Georgia Tech in 1902. The night before the game, the Clemson players stepped off the train, checked in to their hotel and "proceeded to party till dawn," according to one report.

Upon seeing this, the Georgia Tech fans bet heavily on their home team. They figured that the Clemson players would be too exhausted to give their best effort after their big night. Except that the players they were watching were not Clemson's first team—they were just scrubs. The *real* Clemson varsity wiped the field with the Yellow Jackets, 44–5.

Heisman was a strict disciplinarian on and off the field. He allowed players warm showers only after victories.

He insisted that his players keep up their grades or there would be consequences. As one story goes, Clemson's kicker didn't keep up his grades to Heisman's satisfaction, and the coach told him he couldn't play in a game.

The player protested. "Coach, don't you know that the sportswriters call this toe on my right foot the million-dollar toe?"

Replied Heisman, "What good is it if you only have a fifteen-cent head?"

Heisman made his biggest mark at Georgia Tech, where he posted a 100-29-6 record, including a 32-game unbeaten streak. It was in a game against Cumberland University that was one of the most infamous in college football history that Heisman set part of his legacy. For years sportswriters had been selecting national champions based on the total points scored. Schools were running up scores just to get votes for the National Championship.

Heisman felt it was wrong and decided to prove it with a football game against Cumberland, a weak opponent given little chance of beating Georgia Tech. He also wanted revenge for a 22-0 loss in baseball the year before when Cumberland used pro baseball players.

When Cumberland canceled the football game, Heisman threatened to sue for $3,000. He offered a $500 incentive to bring the team to Atlanta. They accepted.

On October 7, 1916, the game began. And there was trouble from the beginning for Cumberland. Georgia Tech scored on the first play. Things quickly got worse for Cumberland. Georgia Tech led 63-0 at the end of the first quarter and 126-0 at halftime.

Heisman's speech at halftime didn't reference the score and had no hint of letting up.

"You're doing all right. But you can't tell what those Cumberland boys have up their sleeves. Be alert, men! Hit 'em clean, but hit 'em hard."

The Cumberland locker room had a different vibe.

"Hang on boys! Remember the $500!"

More than likely, they would remember the still unrivaled score: 222-0.

Georgia Tech scored on the first play. Things quickly got worse for Cumberland. Georgia Tech led 63-0 at the end of the first quarter and 126-0 at halftime.

Heisman continued to coach until 1927, ending a 35-year coaching career. He became athletic director at the Downtown Athletic Club in New York, which began to give out a trophy for the best college football player in the country in 1935.

Heisman died a year later and the trophy was renamed for him as a memorial.

Bending the 21st Century Rules

Cheaters? New England Stretches the Rules

For decades, the New York Yankees were the most hated of sports franchises. Baseball fans despised their free spending from the 1970s onward. Before that, they were jealous of the Bronx Bombers' ability to find Hall of Fame–caliber players seemingly everywhere, or their skills at making lopsided trades.

There's a new Public Enemy Number 1 on the sports landscape this century. Outside of New England, the Patriots unquestionably have taken the place of the Yankees.

Yes, their success—four Super Bowl titles and six trips in the first 15 seasons of the millennium—has caused envy everywhere beyond their rabid fan base. But the hatred for Robert Kraft's team emanates from the perception that the Patriots operate outside of NFL rules. Outside of the parameters of good sportsmanship, too.

Most recently, there was "Deflategate," the over-the-top silliness involving under-the-prescribed-limit of air in the footballs for New England's AFC championship victory over Indianapolis in January 2015. Before that was "Spygate" in 2007, another season in which the Patriots made the Super Bowl.

Assorted other suspicions and conspiracy theories abound, so much so that nearly every opponent of the Patriots becomes ultra-paranoid in the week leading up to facing them on the field. See that guy with the beer belly and binoculars standing under that tree with the box of popcorn in his hand? Could he be performing espionage for Bill Belichick?

New England Patriots head coach Bill Belichick celebrates with quarterback Tom Brady after Super Bowl XLIX.

On Spying on One's Opponent Along with, Well, Everybody

"Eighty thousand people saw it, everybody on the sideline saw it, everybody sees our guys in front of 80,000 people. I mean, there he is. It was wrong, we were disciplined for it, that's it. We never did it again. We're never going to do it again. Anything else that's close, we're not going to do either." —*New England Patriots head coach Bill Belichick*

AUDIBLE

And why do visiting teams' sideline headsets go blooey during games at Gillette Stadium when the Patriots experience little or no such interference?

It all seems so comical; every competitor in every sport seeks an edge. Yet, there is so much Dr. Evil in Belichick's manner, and so much secrecy around the Patriots' compound that breaking the rules seems anything but farfetched in Foxborough.

Plus, there's evidence, particularly in the Spygate case, when Belichick was fined $500,000 for spying on an opponent's defensive signals, the culmination of a scheme that lasted several years. The Patriots organization was fined $250,000 in the case and stripped of their 2008 first-round draft pick.

Belichick eventually made real comments (and admission of guilt) about Spygate.

"A guy is giving signals in front of 80,000 people, OK?" Belichick said. "So we filmed them taking signals in front of 80,000 people—like there were a lot of other teams doing at that time, too. Forget about that. If we were wrong, we've been disciplined for that."

Deflategate was even more absurd. The NFL spent nearly $5 million for an "independent" investigation by attorney Ted Wells, whose report was so full of holes it looked like the expansion Buccaneers' defense. Yet Commissioner Roger Goodell and his staff suspended star quarterback Tom Brady for the first four games of 2015 and nailed the team for $1 million in fines and the forfeiture of a first-round draft selection in 2016, and a fourth-rounder in 2017.

Kraft, long a confidant of the commissioner, reluctantly accepted his punishment—he later regretted the decision when Goodell upheld Brady's suspension in an appeal hearing. Then Brady went to federal court and won, getting the suspension overturned on procedural grounds; the judge never ruled on the evidence and Brady's alleged guilt.

The league was accused by many—and not only Patriots backers—of carrying a vendetta against the franchise. Others claimed the NFL has so much proof that the Patriots covertly have been committing many egregious acts that the league finally got fed up with the "cheating."

Marty Hurney, the general manager of the Carolina Panthers when they fell to the Patriots in the 2004 Super Bowl, felt compelled on his radio show to revisit the circumstances surrounding that game once Deflategate broke.

"There are people who swear to me that the Patriots taped our practice down in Houston during Super Bowl week," Hurney said. "I can't prove it. I don't know. And I hate talking like this because I feel like a bad loser, but it just gnaws at you. . . .

"You go to Spygate after our Super Bowl and things came out about a rumor about a video guy, and he had tapes and he goes to Hawaii and kind of disappears.

"These are all rumors and I can't substantiate any of this. But it gnaws at you."

Regardless, all of the shenanigans involving Belichick's regime have led to some changes: in league rules; in the public's perception of the team and of the NFL; and in the manner in which the media cover America's most popular sport.

Consider:

- The handling of footballs before the games has been altered so that the officiating crews have much more control of their condition.

- Followers of pro football seem to wonder daily what "scandal" might erupt next, whether it emanates from Massachusetts or elsewhere.

The league was accused by many—and not only Patriots backers—of carrying a vendetta against the New England franchise.

- Reporters, particularly those operating in the gonzo journalism genre—even such tabloid entities as ESPN and the various other sports networks/websites fall into the category—seek out the most prurient or sensationalist of angles.

"I find the immediacy of the 24/7 approach to covering the NFL sometimes difficult to adjust to," says Peter King of *Sports Illustrated* and Monday Morning Quarterback, and considered the top journalist covering pro football.

King admits to being "more paranoid about the veracity" of stories and sources than ever. "I think the public exercises righteous indignation when we get something wrong. I have certainly felt that, and rightfully so. But I find fan bases so biased, and often not interested in real reporting."

The Halftime Show

From George Preston Marshall's Invention to Katy Perry's Indoor Flying Act

The buildup to any Super Bowl should focus on the teams playing in the NFL's annual extravaganza. Sometimes, though, it's who is playing when there's no football going on.

Thank the league's marketing folks and network partners for that kind of buzz. Thank U2 for its unforgettable tribute to the victims of the September 11 attacks.

Even thank Janet Jackson and her wardrobe malfunction.

And don't forget to thank George Preston Marshall.

Halftime shows didn't originate with the Washington Redskins owner in the 1930s, but he brought the first elaborate such presentations to the gridiron. Married to an actress, Marshall felt attending an NFL game should be family entertainment and fans should be engrossed for the entire experience. He introduced cheerleaders and a marching band for his spectacles, which included the team's fight song, "Hail to the Redskins," animal acts, circus performers, and symphonies. In December, Santa Claus would make an appearance at halftime. "Football is a game of pageantry," Marshall would say.

Marshall also launched a radio network to carry Redskins games throughout the region. A noted opponent of integration, Marshall envisioned his club as a representative of the South; before games, his band played "Dixie."

Fans in the South also were enjoying their school's marching bands, particularly from traditionally African-American schools such as Florida A&M and Southern University. They boasted with pride (and accuracy) about the rollicking halftime performances.

Madonna played the Super Bowl halftime show in 2012.

Now, every school does so.

Corey Spurlin, director of the Auburn University Marching Band, notes that such college units are a "defining component for the collegiate atmosphere, as distinct from the NFL.

"We are battling a lot of different forms of entertainment, including some collegiate stadiums that feel they need to bring in pop musical talent and blast loud canned music rather than promote their bands," Spurlin says. "This is ironic, because the NFL teams love to get the college bands to their stadiums to perform at halftime. It is almost as if many of the college athletic departments don't realize what a unique component they have to offer college fans.

"We are fortunate at Auburn that we haven't faced that with our athletic department."

Buckeyes supporters flock to Ohio Stadium to see their team romp on the field, and few of them leave their seats without seeing the band dot the i in "Script Ohio."

Even the Stanford band, which believes in creating mayhem as much as in entertaining, has its loyal supporters. The band's mascot, the Stanford Tree, periodically has been banned by the NCAA from appearing.

Still, the showstopper among halftime shows always is the Super Bowl spectacular. At least it has been since 1991 and the 25th edition of the big game.

That Super Bowl is best remembered for Whitney Houston's stirring rendition of the national anthem—the first Gulf War was being fought at that time—and Scott Norwood's wide-right field goal. In celebration of a quarter-century of Super Bowls, the NFL turned over halftime to the folks at Disney, who hired New Kids on the Block (don't laugh, they were big back then).

NFL execs were thrilled with everything in Tampa. They couldn't guarantee more down-to-the-wire finishes, but they could consistently hit the big time at halftime.

"They'd never really gone after real star power," Jim Steeg, who helped establish the NFL's special events department, said of his predecessors at the league. And after the 1992 halftime show starring Gloria Estefan, plus figure skating gold medalists Brian Boitano and Dorothy Hamill in a salute to the upcoming Albertville Olympics, fell victim to counterprogramming on other networks, Steeg knew what was needed.

In celebration of a quarter-century of Super Bowls, the NFL turned over halftime production to the folks at Disney, who hired New Kids on the Block.

For the '93 show at the Rose Bowl, he targeted Michael Jackson. "I remember pitching them," Steeg told *Sports Illustrated*, "and them not really having a clue what we were talking about." Then Jackson was told about the international viewership.

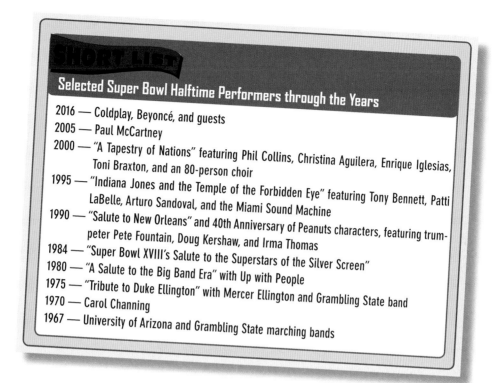

SHORT LIST

Selected Super Bowl Halftime Performers through the Years

2016 — Coldplay, Beyoncé, and guests

2005 — Paul McCartney

2000 — "A Tapestry of Nations" featuring Phil Collins, Christina Aguilera, Enrique Iglesias, Toni Braxton, and an 80-person choir

1995 — "Indiana Jones and the Temple of the Forbidden Eye" featuring Tony Bennett, Patti LaBelle, Arturo Sandoval, and the Miami Sound Machine

1990 — "Salute to New Orleans" and 40th Anniversary of Peanuts characters, featuring trumpeter Pete Fountain, Doug Kershaw, and Irma Thomas

1984 — "Super Bowl XVIII's Salute to the Superstars of the Silver Screen"

1980 — "A Salute to the Big Band Era" with Up with People

1975 — "Tribute to Duke Ellington" with Mercer Ellington and Grambling State band

1970 — Carol Channing

1967 — University of Arizona and Grambling State marching bands

"So you're telling me that this show is going live to all those places where I'll never do a concert?" Jackson said. "I'm in."

And now the NFL was in with the big boys and girls. From Jackson's 3,500-person miniconcert, the roster of entertainers would scale the Everest of show business in the 1980s and '90s.

Jackson's sister, Janet, was scheduled for the 2002 show in New Orleans, but she canceled after the September 11 terrorist attacks. The NFL determined, rightly so, that a patriotic theme would fit best for halftime of the Super Bowl, pushed back one week in February.

About the time of Jackson's withdrawal, the league's John Collins saw U2 perform at Madison Square Garden. The Irish band's encore included the names of those killed in the attacks scrolling across the roof of the Garden.

"At first people didn't know what was going on," Collins told *Sports Illustrated*, "and then you heard, 'Oh, my God!' as they realized. . . . It was . . . an amazing moment."

U2 would replicate that moment in the most moving and memorable halftime performance the Super Bowl has ever seen, and probably ever will see.

ACKNOWLEDGMENTS

The authors would like to thank George Atallah, Judy Battista, Gil Brandt, Joe Browne, Rachel Cohen, Steve Cohen, Tim Dahlberg, Pat Kirwan, Joe Linta, Brian McCarthy, Robbie Mendelson, Paul Montella, Nick Pavlatos, Frank Ramos, Jilane Rodgers, Adam Schein, Michael Signora, Corey Spurlin, Jim Steeg, Jimmy Vaccaro, Mark Waller, Stephen Luke, Jim Summaria, Marianne O'Leary, Jeff Nelson, Kristina Petersen, John Heisler, and Carol Copley.

INDEX

Italicized page numbers
indicate illustrations.

PHOTO CREDITS

"Audible" sidebar illustration by Aaron H. Dana

--

Panel Page, Zeller and Grange: *New York World Telegram & Sun* photo by Alan Fisher, Library of Congress, background: Thinkstockphotos.com; p. v: Farm Security Administration—Office of War Information Photograph Collection, Library of Congress; p. x: Library of Congress; p. xi: The Lyda Hill Texas Collection of Photographs in Carol M. Highsmith's America Project, Library of Congress, Prints and Photographs Division

--

No. 5, TV camera: Photo by J. Glover, Atlanta, Georgia. Own work, CC BY-SA 3.0, https://commons.wikimedia.org/w/index.php?curid=2896593; background: sirandel/iStock/ThinkStock

No. 4, Super Bowl ticket: Photo by Stephen D. Luke

No. 3, Rozelle and Halas: Photo by Jim Summaria; background: iStock/ThinkStock

No. 2, Kenny Washington: *Los Angeles Daily News* Negatives, UCLA Library. Copyright Regents of the University of California, UCLA Library. http://creativecommons.org/licenses/by/4.0/; background: Fuse/ThinkStock

No. 1, Theodore Roosevelt: Library of Congress, background: iStock/ThinkStock; death cartoon: Library of Congress

--

No. 6, Las Vegas sportsbook: https://commons.wikimedia.org/w/index.php?curid=19088094; background: Fuse/ThinkStock

No. 7, Leather helmet: Courtesy of the Gerald R. Ford Presidential Museum; background: iStock/ThinkStock

No. 8, Johnny Unitas: Malcolm Emmons-*USA TODAY* Sports; background: iStock/ThinkStock

No. 9, NFL draft: Photo by Marianne O'Leary. https://creativecommons.org/licenses/by/2.0/

No. 10, Zeller and Grange: *New York World Telegram & Sun* photo by Alan Fisher, Library of Congress; background: iStock/ThinkStock

No. 11, Gatorade bath: Tommy Gilligan-*USA TODAY* Sports; background: iStock/ThinkStock

No. 12, Walter Camp: Manuscripts and Archives, Yale University Library; background: iStock/ThinkStock

No. 13, Red Grange: Library of Congress

No. 14, Gil Brandt: Matthew Emmons-*USA TODAY* Sports

No. 15, Packers fans: Photographs in the Carol M. Highsmith Archive, Library of Congress, Prints and Photographs Division

No. 16, Referee review: Photo by Brian Cantoni. https://creativecommons.org/licenses by/2.0/; background: iStock/ThinkStock

No. 17, Rose Bowl: Kirby Lee-*USA TODAY* Sports

No. 18, Roger Goodell: Photo by Marianne O'Leary
No. 19, Joe Namath, Los Angeles Rams: Darryl Norenberg-*USA TODAY* Sports
No. 20, Oakland Raiders: Darryl Norenberg-*USA TODAY* Sports
No. 21, Camera crew: Photo by Thomson20192. https://creativecommons.org/licenses by/2.0/; background: sirandel/iStock/ThinkStock
No. 22, Blue turf: By Bsuorangecrush (talk)—I (Bsuorangecrush [talk]) created this work entirely by myself. CC BY-SA 3.0, https://en.wikipedia.org/w/index.php?curid=30021682; background: iStock/ThinkStock
No. 23, Alabama mascot: The George F. Landegger Collection of Alabama Photographs in Carol M. Highsmith's America, Library of Congress, Prints and Photographs Division
No. 24, Alonzo Stagg photographs: Library of Congress; background: Jupiterimages/PHOTOs.com/ThinkStock
No. 25, Paul Brown: David Boss-*USA TODAY* Sports
No. 26, Four Horsemen and Knute Rockne: Library of Congress; background: Fuse/ThinkStock
No. 27, Jimmy Jones: Darryl Norenberg-*USA TODAY* Sports; background: iStock/ThinkStock
No. 28, Joe Namath fur coat: Joe Camporeale-*USA TODAY* Sports
No. 29, Lightning strike: efks/iStock/Thinkstock
No. 30, Georgetown-Carlisle game and Pop Warner: Library of Congress
No. 31, Joe Montana: Manny Rubio-*USA TODAY* Sports
No. 32, Patriots offense: Photo by Stephen D. Luke; background: iStock/ThinkStock
No. 33, Lombardi Trophy: Photo by Stephen D. Luke
No. 34, DeMaurice F. "De" Smith: By NFL Players Association—Own work, GFDL, https://commons.wikimedia.org/w/index.php?curid=10537487; background: iStock/ThinkStock
No. 35, Joe Paterno: Penn State Atlhetics
No. 36, Paul Bear Bryant: Manny Rubio-*USA TODAY* Sports
No. 37, Joe Flacco: Photo by Keith Allison. https://creativecommons.org/licenses/by-sa/2.0/; background: iStock/ThinkStock
No. 38, Sammy Baugh: Library of Congress
No. 39, Cowboys platoon: The Lyda Hill Texas Collection of Photographs in Carol M. Highsmith's America Project, Library of Congress, Prints and Photographs Division
No. 40, Eddie Robinson: RVR Photos-*USA TODAY* Sports
No. 41, Sid Gillman: Darryl Norenberg-*USA TODAY* Sports
No. 42, Steelers defense: By SteelCityHobbies - MRR_0028, CC BY 2.0, https://commons.wikimedia.org/w/index.php?curid=4489165; background: AlbertoChagas/iStock/ThinkStock
No. 43, Deacon Jones: Malcolm Emmons-*USA TODAY* Sports
No. 44, Jim Parker: Darryl Norenberg-*USA TODAY* Sports
No. 45, Princeton-Rutgers: Manuscripts and Archives, Yale University Library; background: iStock/ThinkStock

No. 46, Miami-Oakland in London: Photo by daniel0685. https://creativecommons.org/licenses/by/2.0/

No. 47, Pete Gogolak: Dick Raphael-*USA TODAY* Sports

No. 48, Georgia Tech and John Heisman: Wikimedia Commons; background: Jupiterimages/PHOTOs
.com/ThinkStock

No. 49, Bill Belichick and Tom Brady: Mark J. Rebilas-*USA TODAY* Sports

No. 50, Madonna halftime show: Photo by Stephen D. Luke; background: sirandel/iStock/ThinkStock

ABOUT THE AUTHORS

Barry Wilner has been a sportswriter for The Associated Press since 1975. He has covered virtually every major sporting event, including 13 Olympics, 9 World Cups, 30 Super Bowls, the World Series, and the Stanley Cup finals, and has written more than fifty books. He is also an adjunct professor at Manhattanville College. He lives with his wife, Helene, in Garnerville, New York.

Ken Rappoport is the author of nearly seventy sports books for adults and young readers. While working for The Associated Press in New York for thirty years, he has written about every major sport. His assignments have included the World Series, the NBA Finals, and, as the AP's national hockey writer, the Stanley Cup Finals and the Olympics. He lives in Egg Harbor Township, New Jersey.

ALSO BY KEN RAPPOPORT AND BARRY WILNER

Super Bowl Heroes, Lyons Press
On the Clock, Taylor Trade Publishing
Crazyball, Taylor Trade Publishing
The Big Dance—The story of the NCAA basketball tournament, Taylor Trade Publishing
The Little League That Could, Taylor Trade Publishing
Penn State Football—The Complete Illustrated History, MVP Books
Harvard Beats Yale 29-29, Taylor Trade Publishing
Football Feuds, Lyons Press
Miracles, Shockers and Long Shots, Taylor Trade Publishing
Gridiron Glory, Taylor Trade Publishing
Villains, Andrews McMeel
Girls Rule!, Andrews McMeel
They Changed the Game, Andrews McMeel